SPIRALGUIDE

AA

Publishing

OLAND

Contents

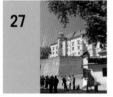

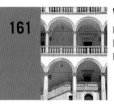

Written by Marc Di Duca
Verified by Mark Baker

Series editor Karen Rigden
Designed by Liz Baldin of Bookwork Creative Associates Ltd.

Published by AA Publishing, a trading name of Automobile
Association Developments Limited, whose registered office
is Fanum House, Basing View, Basingstoke, Hampshire RG21 4EA.
Registered number 1878835.

ISBN: 978-0-7495-6138-3

The contents of this publication are believed correct at the time
of printing. Nevertheless, AA Publishing accept no responsibility
for errors, omissions or changes in the details given, or for the
consequences of readers' reliance on this information. This does not
affect your statutory rights. Assessments of the attractions, hotels and
restaurants are based upon the author's own experience and contain
subjective opinions that may not reflect the publisher's opinion or a
reader's experience. We have tried to ensure accuracy, but things do
change, so please let us know if you have any comments or corrections.

A CIP catalogue record for this book is available from the British
Library

© Automobile Association Developments Limited 2009
Maps © Automobile Association Developments Limited 2009

Cover design and binding style by permission of AA Publishing
Colour separation by Leo Reprographics
Printed and bound in China by Leo Paper Products

Find out more about AA Publishing and the wide range of services the
AA provides by visiting our Web site at www.theAA.com/bookshop

A03607
Maps in this title produced from data supplied by Global Mapping,
Brackley, UK
Copyright © Global Mapping/Daunpol
Transport map © Communicarta Ltd, UK

The Magazine

A great holiday is more than just lying on a beach or shopping till you drop – to really get the most from your trip you need to know what makes the place tick. The Magazine provides an entertaining overview to some of the social, cultural and natural elements that make up the unique character of this engaging country.

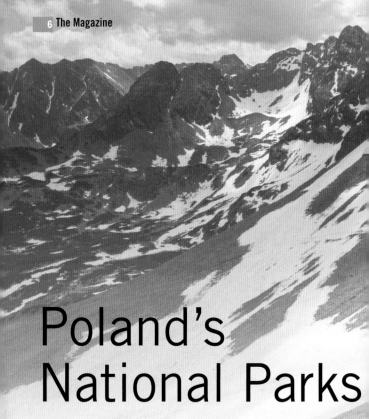

Poland's National Parks

From the heights of the Tatra Mountains to the dunes of the Baltic Sea and from the deep forests of Białwieża to canyons and cliffs near Kraków, Poland has an incredibly diverse array of national parks which shelter some of the most precious habitats in Europe.

WILD POLAND

Though covering a mere one per cent of the country's area (315,000 hectares/778,050 acres), Poland's 23 national parks protect very diverse and unspoiled landscapes and geographical features. These include dunes along the Baltic coast, marshes, wetlands and forests in the east and mountain ranges in the south, all of which are home to thousands of species of flora and fauna. Wherever you travel in the country, you are never far from a national park, and even Warsaw has the Kampinoski National Park's dunes and forests virtually on its doorstep. All protected areas are open to visitors but conservation of habitats and protection of

MOUNTAINS AND HIGHLANDS

- **Babiogorski** – Smallest in the country; limited to one mountain south of Kraków
- **Bieszczadzki** - World Biosphere Reserve in far southeastern corner of Poland
- **Gorczański** – Dense forest of the Gorce Mountains near Nowy Targ
- **Karkonoski** – Mountain range along the Czech-Polish border
- **Magurski** – Forested highlands on the border with Slovakia
- **Ojców ski** – Canyons and limestone cliffs to the north of Kraków
- **Pieniński** – Tiny park around the Dunajec River Gorge on the border with Slovakia
- **Roztoczański** – southeast of Zamość
- **Stołowe Mountains** – Age-old flat-top mountains in the south
- **Świętokrzyski** – Low mountain range near Kielce
- **Tatrzanski** - Tatra Mountains on the border with Slovakia

he specific character of the location always take precedence over visitors. This usually means there are rules to be followed such as no overnight camping, starting fires and the like. The most popular parks are the Białowiża National Park (▶ 66–67), straddling the Belarusian border and famous for its European bison, and the Tatrzanski National Park in the Tatra Mountains of the south. Other parks you may like to visit for hiking and nature watching include the Karkonoski National Park, the Stołowe Mountains and the coastal Słowiński National Park near Gdańsk.

Above: Białowieski is the oldest national park in Poland and a UNESCO World Heritage Site. Page 5: Canal-side architecture in Gdansk. Pages 6–7: The Tatra Mountains

LOWLANDS, FORESTS, LAKES, RIVERS AND WETLANDS

- **Białowieski** - On the border with Belarus, famous for its bison population
- **Biebrzanski** – Largest park in the country, which protects wetlands northeast of Białystok
- **Bory Tucholskie** – Lakes and wetlands north of Chojnice
- **Drawienski** – Drawa primeval forest along the River Drawa
- **Kampinoski** – Sand dunes and forest northwest of Warsaw
- **Narwiański** – Marsh and river habitats west of Białystok
- **Poleski** – Tiny wetland park northeast of Lublin
- **Ujście Warty** – Important bird habitat on the German border
- **Wielkopolski** – On the southern outskirts of Poznań
- **Wigierski** – Lakes and forests east of Suwałki

BALTIC COAST

- **Słowiński** – Coastal park of dunes, forest and water to the west of Gdańsk
- **Wolinski** – Small coastal park near the northwest city of Świnoujście

Temples to Timber
Poland's wooden churches

From the Tatra Mountains to the Ukrainian border, fairy-tale timber churches dot southern Poland's rural uplands. Built between the 15th and 19th centuries, these UNESCO-protected structures are among Poland's most remarkable architectural features.

WHY WOOD?

Landowners in southern Poland realised that wood had many advantages over stone when it came to church building. It was readily available in the mountains, cheaper and lighter, and carpenters could erect a large church much more quickly than masons could in stone. Resilient larch wood, almost as hard as stone when dried, is the main material used, though pine, yew, spruce, oak and beech churches can also be found.

WHERE TO LOOK?

Possibly the best example can be seen in Haczów, which boasts the world's largest timber Gothic church. Others are in Dębno Podhalańskie and the areas around Muszyna, Binarowa, Blizne, Lipnica Murowana and Sękowa. In Małopolska a trail extends for 1,500km (930 miles) linking one church to the next.

Above: Exterior decoration on a church in Debno. Right: Exterior of the wooden Church of St Clement in Zakopane

Lech Wałęsa rose from shipyard electrician to Poland's president in the 1980s

The Solidarity
MOVEMENT

Today's Poles owe much to *Solidarność*, a broad-ranging movement which did more than any other to challenge Communist rule during the Cold War. Solidarity's actions in the early 1980s constituted the first cracks in the Communist wall, which eventually came tumbling down at the end of the decade. The best-known figure to emerge from the movement was Lech Wałęsa, a Gdańsk shipyard electrician who became the country's first post-Communist president.

EARLY STRIKES

In summer 1980, following a decade of economic woes and disquiet, a decision by the authorities to raise meat prices in workers' canteens caused a wave of strikes to break out across Poland, most notably bringing the southern coal mines and the Lenin Shipyard in Gdańsk to a standstill. The Communists found themselves forced to agree to Lech Wałęsa's demand that the Poles be given the right to form independent trade unions. Solidarity was established on 17 September and by 1981 it had grown into an organisation of 9.5 million members, including Catholics, disgruntled Communists and those demanding democracy.

MARTIAL LAW

The year 1981 was difficult in Poland. Strikes and skirmishes with the security forces continued for most of the year, especially in the northeastern town of Bydgoszcz. Popular Lech Wałęsa was elected president of Solidarity in September, but dark days were ahead for both him and Solidarity. During the night of 12–13 December, General Wojciech Jaruzelski, First Secretary of the Communist Party and Polish Prime Minister, declared martial law across Poland and many activists were rounded up. Strikes were met with brutal repression, and nine miners were killed in Katowice. Things got so bad that Pope John Paul II appealed for an end to the bloodshed in his homeland, but the next year witnessed more strikes and violence, until the Communists, thinking that Solidarity had been crushed, decided to suspend martial law in December 1982.

MID-80S THAW

In 1983, much to the annoyance of the Communist regime, Lech Wałęsa was awarded the Nobel Peace Prize but otherwise there was little reason for optimism in Poland in the face of a worsening economic situation and with hundreds of Solidarity members in prison. However, with Mikhail

The Solidarity movement became much than a trade union under Wałęsa's leadership

Gorbachev's arrival on the scene in Moscow in 1985, a thaw set in across the Eastern Bloc. An amnesty was declared for Solidarity members and the union began slowly to re-form. In 1988 Polish interior minister, General Czesław Kiszczak, proposed a meeting between Solidarity, the Church and the government – often called the Round Table negotiations – during which it was decided to hold the first free elections in the Eastern Bloc.

TIMELINE

10th century: Piast unites Slav clans around Poznań.

1038: Kraków established as capital.

1226: Teutonic knights overrun north from their base at Malbork.

1569: Poles unite with Lithuanians to form Europe's largest country.

1596: Capital moved from Kraków to Warsaw.

1655–60: Swedish invasion known as "the Deluge".

Late 18th century: Poland divided between Prussia, Russia and Austria.

1918: Poland reappears on the map of Europe

with Józef Piłsudski as head of state.

1939: Hitler invades Poland to begin World War II.

1941–5: Atrocities committed at concentration camps such as Auschwitz and Treblinka.

ROADS TO FREEDOM

Anyone interested in the Solidarity movement shouldn't miss Gdańsk's "Roads to Freedom" exhibition. The exhibition not only tells the Solidarity story but also provides a lot of background on life in Poland during the 1970s and 1980s using a mock-up of a period grocery store, period films including Jaruzelski's TV declaration of martial law and many other fascinating exhibits. The exhibition is currently housed at Solidarity headquarters at ul. Wały Piastowskie 24 but it is planned to move it back to the Gdańsk shipyard in 2010.

POWER TO THE PEOPLE

The June elections of 1989 saw Lech Wałęsa's Citizen's Committee win almost 100 per cent of the seats in both houses of parliament. The Polish Communist Party dissolved itself and Wałęsa became Poland's first post-Communist president. The effect this had on the rest of Eastern Europe was electric: by late autumn totalitarian regimes from the German border to the Black Sea had fallen like dominoes.

TODAY

Lech Wałęsa went on to serve as Polish President until 1995 but fell out of favour with the electorate. He now travels the world, receiving awards and giving lectures and occasionally still comments on events in his homeland. The Solidarity phenomenon went the way of almost all mass political umbrella movements in late 1980s Eastern Europe, fracturing into several smaller parties who now squabble among themselves.

1943: Jewish Ghetto uprising in Warsaw.

1944: Failed Warsaw popular uprising against the Nazis.

1945: Red Army liberates Poland, which falls into Soviet sphere of influence.

1947: Communist party comes to power and begins process of Sovietisation.

1978: Archbishop of Kraków, Karol Wojtyła, becomes Pope John Paul II.

1980: Solidarity movement founded; first chairman is Lech Wałęsa.

1981: Martial law declared in Poland by General Jaruzelski.

1989: First semi-free election in Eastern Bloc following Round Table negotiation between the Church, Solidarity and state.

1990: Communist party dissolved. Lech Wałęsa becomes president.

2004: Poland joins the EU.

Raise Your Spirits!

Poles and their vodka

Enter any shop or supermarket in Poland and somewhere among the aisles you will be confronted by a wall of sparkling bottles, some crystal clear, others one of a rainbow of colours, but all containing Poland's tipple of choice – vodka.

Poles are just as passionate about their *Wódka* (as it is known in Polish) as their more notorious spirit-loving Russian and Ukrainian neighbours to the east. It was originally used for medicinal purposes as long ago as the 8th century, but the Slavs soon discovered that imbibing the 40 per cent proof concoction had various other desirable effects. Among hundreds of different brands, Żubrówka, infused with bison grass according to a centuries-old recipe, is probably the best known and a common souvenir item taken home by tourists. This is often mixed with apple juice to create a cocktail called a *szarlotka* or *tatanka*. Most Poles, however, prefer their favourite firewater straight, although since the fall of Communism concoctions infused with lemon, peach, juniper berries, honey and even cannabis have appeared on shop shelves.

VODKA ETIQUETTE

Vodka drinking is no wild free-for-all in Eastern Europe – there is a definite ritual and order to inebriation, which must be strictly obeyed. After your glass is filled, wait until the host has said a toast, then down the contents

in one, *do dna,* as the Poles say, no sipping or saving half for later. Follow this with a little piece of something – gherkin, bread, morsel of cheese. Glasses loaded again, second toast and down the hatch, little nibble, and again, and again…

POLISH PINTS

Those who dislike strong spirits will be happy to learn that many young Poles are drinking less vodka these days and turning instead to less intoxicating beer. Very quaffable brands to look out for include Żywiec, Warka, Tyskie, Okocim and Lech, most of which have long been available abroad. Whatever your tipple, *na zdrowie!*

Clockwise from top left: Flavoured vodkas for sale in Kraków; locals enjoy their vodka neat; nightlife isn't just all about bars; the popularity of beer in young Poles is increasing

THE GÓRALE

The Tatra and Beskid Highlanders

The Carpathian Mountains arch across Eastern Europe from Romania to Slovakia and are inhabited by traditional peoples bearing different names but sharing many similar cultural traits, which are shaped by the mountain environment they inhabit. Poland's Górale or Highlanders are independent-minded folk found in the Tatra and Beskid mountain ranges of Southern Poland. To visit a Górale village, festival or wedding is to experience living Polish folk culture at its most colourful.

Cut off from mainstream culture and foreign influence for centuries, the Górale are an ethnically distinct group numbering some 600,000 and thought to be descended from migrating Balkan shepherds. Possibly the one aspect of their culture that sets them apart from their plain-dwelling compatriots is their dialect, which Poles can understand but which includes many words not found in standard Polish. Górale is a general name used to describe numerous different groups, and language differs slightly from village to village, as do costume, cuisine and music.

GÓRALE LIFE

Highland culture comes in many guises – from traditional carved timber furniture to folk costume to the Górales' distinctive flute and strings music. The Górale like their food calorie-packed, and dishes containing ewe's cheese, potatoes, sauerkraut, mutton and oscypek (smoked sheep's milk cheese), common ingredients available in the alpine environment, feature heavily in recipes. Traditional Górale abodes are plain log structures with chunky wooden furniture arranged around a decorated stove, and their simple attire includes cotton blouses, embroidered pinafores, felt hats, thick woollen socks, sheepskin slippers and woollen shawls, all of which make colourful souvenirs.

FOLK CULTURE

The Podhale area and the Tatra Mountains around the towns of Nowy Targ and Zakopane are naturally the best places to see Highlanders in the flesh. However, thanks to a revival of folk culture across Poland, distinctive mountain culture can now be enjoyed across the land. Mock Carpathian restaurants with live music have popped up from Kraków to Gdańsk, and Górale can be encountered behind market stalls in big cities, touting their traditional wares. Tatra song and whirling dance are often the centrepieces of Polish folk festivals, though by far the best event to catch is still the Festival of Mountain Folklore in August in Zakopane, which draws not only Górale folk ensembles but also mountain people from all over the world.

The beautiful Tatra Mountains, home to the Górale who live traditional and simple lives

IF THESE WALLS COULD TALK
Architectural Styles

Poland's diverse architectural heritage is the result of a thousand years of artistic influence, invasion and folk tradition. Although a huge number of original structures were destroyed during World War II, the post-war period witnessed reconstruction on an unparalleled scale.

ROMANESQUE

Poland's oldest buildings date back to the days of the country's earliest Slav rulers (from the 10th to the 13th century). Understandably, few examples from this period have survived.

Highlights

- St Adalbert's Church (right), Kraków
- St Andrew's Church, Kraków (➤ 83)
- St Prokop's Church, Strzelno

GOTHIC

Gothic is the dominant style in Poland and almost every town possesses a typical redbrick church or cathedral complete with trademark elongated windows, pointed arches and lofty vaulted ceilings. Size mattered in the Gothic period, and some buildings dating from the 14th to the 16th century reached gargantuan proportions.

Highlights

- Malbork Castle (right), (➤ 146)
- St Mary's Church, Gdańsk
- Basilica of SS Peter and Paul, Poznań

RENAISSANCE

A new Italian-inspired style took over in the 16th century and placed the focus firmly on decoration and proportion in stark contrast to Gothic's bare bricks and towering edifices. Architects of the day used stucco, sgraffito, turrets, ornate gables, parapets and other decorative elements to create striking buildings and sometimes even entire towns such as Zamość.

Highlights

- Zamość town centre (➤ 104)
- Castle at Baranów Sandomierski (➤ 113)
- Wawel Castle (right), Kraków (➤ 84)

BAROQUE

Decorative baroque first appeared in Poland in the 17th century and although it soon took hold. Many existing churches, palaces and castles were given a baroque cladding of swirling stucco, pipe-playing cherubs and over-the-top gilt ornament.

Highlights

- Church of St Anne, Kraków
- Lubiąż Monastery (right)
- Aula Leopoldina, Wrocław

NEO STYLES

In the 19th century architects revisited architectural styles of the past which resulted in a large number of neo-Gothic, neo-Renaissance and neoclassical buildings. Neoclassicism demanded symmetry and many buildings took on the look of Greek and Roman temples. Poland's Gothic redbrick style of church building was also revived.

Highlights

- St Catherine's Church (right), Toruń (neo-Gothic)
- Hotel Bristol, Warsaw (neo-Renaissance) (➤ 47, 52)
- Teatr Wielki, Warsaw (neoclassical)

20TH CENTURY

Art nouveau, modernism, functionalism, socialist realism and contemporary styles all left their mark on Poland's cityscapes during the 20th century. Glass-and-steel skyscrapers and shopping malls have done little to enhance Poland's cities since the fall of Communism.

Highlights

- Palace of Science and Culture, Warsaw (socialist realism) (➤ 50)
- Centennial Hall, Wrocław (modernism)
- Arka Pana Church, Nowa Huta (1970s)

BALTIC BELIEFS
Religion in Poland

A red brick church on every old street corner, throngs of pilgrims clogging major religious sites, nuns hurrying across cobbled squares, and congregations so large they spill onto the pavements outside churches – you don't have to be in Poland long to see at first hand just what a devoutly Catholic nation this is. Faith plays a major role in everyday life as well as in politics and in the nation's history, even surviving the repressions of the Communist decades.

Picture the scene – it's Palm Sunday in the small town of Płock and the streets are teeming with groups of teenagers, each led by a priest in full black smock. Some youngsters bear huge gaudily decorated, almost abstract, home-made palms and all are making their way slowly to the cathedral where a group of scruffy tech guys are struggling to set up a huge TV screen and carrying sound equipment into the building. Soon the crowds begin to build up outside, a band strikes up in the nave, the screen flickers on, and the bishop arrives to bless the palms. Speeches giving thanks are made and readings from the bible echo inside while the crowd outside, which would fill the nave twice over, watches events eagerly on the big screen. Between the speeches a choir praising Jesus, the Virgin Mary and Poland joins the band. An hour later the big Palm Sunday day out climaxes in a long procession to the main square where it erupts into a huge party with bands and dancing until late into the evening.

This is just a single event in one small town, but shows just how powerful a force the Church (if not religion) is in Poland. Contrast this with Poland's neighbour, the Czech Republic, once as devout but now a place where hardly anyone under 60 enters a church for religious reasons.

PIOUS POWER
Since the political changes of the late 1980s, the role of the Church in society has grown stronger and its influence in politics has increased.

Church of Our Lady in Lichen – just one of the grand Catholic churches to be found in Poland

Its standpoint on issues such as abortion, same-sex partnerships and religious education in schools has often been controversial, as has its influence on political parties such as the Law and Justice Party or the League of Polish Families. Some in Poland now think the Church has overstepped the mark, that there are too many churches and priests and that funds could be spent more wisely.

JOHN PAUL II

One of the greatest outpourings of religious fervour in recent years followed the death of Pope John Paul II, understandably a much-loved figure throughout his pontiffship and a candle in the dark night of Communism for many Catholics, not only in Poland. Since his death countless roads, squares, bridges, ring roads and roundabouts have been named in his honour and statues of his likeness have sprouted like mushrooms after summer rain.

The death of Pope John Paul II was felt by the whole country

TEN MILLION PILGRIMS' TALES

It's reckoned that Poland's pilgrimage sites receive around 10 million faithful every year. The most popular pilgrimage destinations are the Jasna Góra Monastery in Częstochowa (► 111), the Basilica of Our Lady in Licheń (► 154) and the Kalwaria Zebrzydowska, which heave year-round with school parties, priest youth club leaders, nuns, and the odd bewildered tourist. The power of these places is immense and it's difficult not to get swept away with the fervour, especially at major festivals such as Easter and the Feast of the Assumption.

BLACK SHEEP OF POLAND'S FLOCK

Catholics may form an overwhelming majority but around 5 per cent of Poles subscribe to other denominations and faiths. The Uniate Church

MUSLIMS OF EASTERN POLAND

Some 75 per cent of Poles are Catholics but not in the eastern villages of Kruszyniany and Bohoniki. Here the descendants of Tatars who rode with Genghis Khan across the steppe from Central Asia to sack the great cities of Russia and central Europe can be found worshipping in their small timber mosques. Their ancestors, who converted to Islam in the Crimea, were awarded land in eastern Poland by King Jan Sobieski for their part in the defeating the Turks at the Battle of Vienna in 1683.

was formed when the Polish Orthodox Church broke away from Russian Orthodoxy and swore allegiance to Rome but maintained its Slavic Orthodox liturgy. Uniate congregations are generally made up of Poles from areas of Belarus and Ukraine that were once Polish soil, as are those of the Eastern Orthodox Church. Poland also has a tiny indigenous Muslim population.

Crowds at Jasna Góra Monastery to worship The Black Madonna

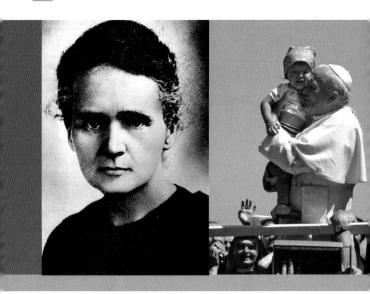

POLES APART

In April 2008, Robert Kubica took pole position at the
Bahrain Formula One Grand Prix, thus becoming the latest in
a long line of Poles to break onto the international scene.

CHURCH AND STATE

Arguably the most famous Pole of all was Pope John Paul II, born Karol
Józef Wojtyła in the small town of Wadowice 50km (31 miles) southeast
of Kraków. In 1978, he became the first non-Italian pope for 450 years
but, more importantly, acted throughout his time as pope as a vocal
critic of Communism in Poland and across Eastern Europe. When he
died in April 2005, all of Poland mourned and candles still burn in his
memory. Throughout much of John Paul II's time at the Vatican, the best
known political leader in his homeland was Lech Wałęsa who became the
country's post-Communist president in the 1990s (► 10–13).

From left to right: Marie Curie; Pope John Paul II; Roman Polański

THE APPLIANCE OF SCIENCE

Nicolaus Copernicus (Mikołaj Kopernik in Polish) was born in Toruń in 1473, and thanks to his theory that the earth orbits the Sun and not the other way round, as had been believed up to that point, he is described by the Poles as "the man who stopped the Sun and moved the Earth". Another celebrated scientific genius was Warsaw's Marie Curie (born Marie Skłodowska in 1867) who first isolated the elements radium and polonium (named after her homeland) and won Nobel prizes for both physics and chemistry.

MEN OF NOTES, LETTERS AND SILVER SCREEN

Born in the small village of Żelazowa Wola near Warsaw in 1849, Fryderyk Chopin was a virtuoso pianist and composer and easily Poland's most illustrious musical personality. In the world of literature, 19th-century Romantic poet Adam Mickiewicz is still compulsory reading for all Polish schoolchildren while Joseph Conrad (born Józef Korzeniowski) is well known to Western readers. Possibly the most celebrated Pole in the world of culture today is Roman Polański (born in Paris to Polish parents), famous for films such as *The Pianist* and *Chinatown*.

THE POLE IN POLE

So what of racing driver, Robert Kubica? Is he destined to take pole position on the grid of famous Poles of our time? Only time will tell.

DID YOU KNOW...?

From golden amber to real gold in liqueurs – here are few things you probably didn't know about Poland.

...that there are so many Poles in Chicago that it is sometimes called Poland's second city?

...that the Ukraine and Poland will be joint hosts of the Euro 2012 soccer championships? Matches will be played in Warsaw, Gdańsk, Wrocław and Poznań but the final is set to take place in the Ukrainian capital Kiev. Preparations for the event have set the country a major challenge but should see Poland's crumbling infrastructure modernised just in time for the arrival of tens of thousands of fans and journalists.

...that there are 9,000 lakes in Poland? In Europe only Finland has more.

...that some 75 per cent of Poles are Roman Catholics?

...that amber found on the Baltic coast is fossilised tree resin formed around 50 million years ago? Many pieces contain leaves, twigs and seeds and even whole insects. Only around 15 per cent of the amber on sale in Poland comes from Polish shores, the rest hailing from the Russian enclave of Kaliningrad.

...that the president and prime minister of Poland from 2006 to 2007 were twins, the Kaczyński brothers Lech and Jarosław?

...that Goldwasser, a liqueur from Gdańsk, contains real flakes of gold leaf?

...that the Polish constitution of 3 May 1791 was the first written document of its kind in Europe and the second in the world after the United States?

Amber is a popular souvenir and most examples on sale are from Polish shores

Finding Your Feet

First Two Hours

Arriving by Air

Poland's main international air gateway is Warsaw's Frederic Chopin Airport and there are other major airports in Kraków and Gdańsk. Most travellers from Europe fly directly to the city they are visiting and there is little need to go via Warsaw unless travelling from another continent with your own national airline or LOT, the Polish flag carrier.

Warsaw

■ Warsaw Airport is located in the suburb of Okęcie, 10km (6 miles) south of the city centre.

■ **Facilities in the arrivals hall** include several *kantors* (bureaux de change), ATMs (cash machines), a tourist information point and news kiosks.

■ To reach central Warsaw by public transport take city bus 175, which runs to the Old Town. Tickets cost 2.40PLN and are available from news kiosks and the tourist information point (or 3PLN from the driver). These must be validated in machines on board. The journey takes around 25 minutes and the service operates frequently from around 5am until 11pm.

■ A licenced **taxi to central Warsaw** from outside the arrivals hall will cost around 25PLN to 30PLN. Avoid unlicensed minicabs that charge many times this amount.

Kraków

■ Kraków Balice Airport is located 11km (7 miles) west of the city centre.

■ **Facilities in the arrivals hall** include a 24-hour *kantor* (bureau de change), ATMs (cash machines), a tourist information point and news kiosks.

■ There are two ways to reach central Kraków by public transport. The simplest way is to take the train to Kraków Główny station. A shuttle bus runs to the airport rail terminal where tickets (6PLN) for the 15-minute trip can be purchased. City bus 192 runs to the city centre. Tickets (2.50PLN) are available from newsagents and the journey takes approximately 40 minutes.

■ A licensed **taxi to central Kraków** from outside the arrivals hall will cost around 60PLN to 70PLN. Again, avoid unofficial taxis.

Gdańsk

■ Gdańsk Lech Wałęsa Airport can be found 14km (9 miles) west of the city centre.

■ **Facilities in the arrivals hall** include several *kantors* (bureaux de change), ATMs, a tourist information point, a bank and news kiosks.

■ City bus B runs to the city centre. Tickets (2.80PLN) are available from the tourist information point and airport newsagents. The journey takes approximately 35 minutes when traffic is light and the service terminates outside Gdańsk Główny railway station.

■ A **taxi to central Gdańsk** from outside the arrivals hall will cost in the region of 50PLN depending on how long the vehicle waits in traffic.

Airport information

Warsaw Tel: 022 650 4220; www.lotnisko-chopina.pl
Kraków Tel: 012 295 5800; www.lotnisko-balice.pl
Gdańsk Tel: 058 348 11 63; www.airport.gdansk.pl
Wrocław Tel: 071 358 1381; www.airport.wroclaw.pl
Poznań Tel: 061 849 2343; www.airport-poznan.com.pl

Arriving by Land

■ There are land **border crossings** with the Czech Republic, Germany, Russia (Kaliningrad Enclave), Lithuania, Belarus, Ukraine and Slovakia.

■ All of Poland's neighbours except Russia, Ukraine and Belarus are members of the EU and the Schengen zone, as is Poland itself, meaning travellers no longer face passport and customs checks on these borders. However, checks can still be carried out anywhere within the country by customs officers and police.

■ Travellers crossing to and from Russia, Belarus and Ukraine face some delays and thorough checks on vehicles and luggage. EU citizens need a visa to enter Russia and Belarus but not for Ukraine.

■ If you are **bringing your own car**, you will need to show a driving licence, an insurance certificate and proof of registration or ownership of the vehicle.

Arriving by Sea

Car and passenger ferries from Sweden and Denmark dock at the ports of Świnoujście, Gdańsk and Gdynia. Services are operated by Stena Line and Polferries. The small Żegluga Gdańska company operates passenger boats to the Russian enclave of Kaliningrad. There are no scheduled services between Poland's coastal cities.

Tourist Information Offices

Almost every town has a tourist information office operated by the local municipal authority or a private company. These are very often located in or near places of interest such as an old town gate or in the town hall itself. Big cities often have several information points in the city centre, the local airport and the main railway station. Staff must speak good English and are usually very helpful indeed. Offices can supply you with free maps, brochures and other information such as bus and rail timetables, accommodation details and restaurant listings. Most also sell maps, guides and souvenirs.

Warsaw
✉ ul. Krakowskie Przedmieście 39
☎ 022 9431;
www.warsawtour.pl

Wrocław
✉ Rynek 14
☎ 071 344 3111;
www.wroclaw.pl

Kraków
✉ Rynek Główny 1 (town hall)
☎ 012 433 7310;
www.krakow.pl

Poznań
✉ ul. Ratajczaka 44
☎ 061 851 9645;
www.poznan.pl

Gdańsk
✉ ul. Długa 45
☎ 058 301 6096;
www.gdansk.pl

Zamość
✉ Rynek Wielki 13 (Town Hall)
☎ 084 639 2292;
www.zamosc.pl

Admission Charges

The cost of admission to museums and other places of interest featured in this guide is indicated by the following price categories.

Inexpensive under 5PLN   **Moderate** 5PLN–12PLN   **Expensive** over 12PLN

Getting Around

By Air

The Polish national airline LOT operates scheduled domestic flights between Warsaw and most major cities.

Driving in Poland

- **Drivers bringing their own car** need to show a driving licence, an insurance certificate and proof of registration or ownership of the vehicle.
- **Car rental** is available at airports and in all of Poland's main cities and large towns. You must be over 21 and have a passport, driving licence and a credit card. Most rental agencies require you to have held your licence for at least one, and sometimes two, years.
- For the **best deals** book in advance online with one of the major international chains (▶ below). Local companies sometimes offer more competitive rates but you should check carefully the level of insurance cover and excess, the technical condition of the vehicle and where you can return it.
- You should keep your passport, driving licence and **vehicle documents with you at all times**, and never leave them unattended in the car. Theft from, and of, vehicles is all too common in Poland.
- If using your own **SatNav**, make sure you update your maps just before you leave as changes to Poland's road network are frequent and road building is ongoing.
- The best Polish **map** series are produced by Demart and Copernicus and are available from all EMPiK bookstores in almost every town and city.

Car Rental Agencies
Budget: www.budget.pl
Europcar: www.europcar.pl
Hertz: www.hertz.pl
National: www.nationalcar.com.pl
Sixt: www.sixt.pl

Driving Essentials
- **Drive on the right.**
- **Seat belts** are compulsory for driver and all passengers, if fitted.
- **Children under 12** (or under 1.5m/4ft 10in tall) must sit in the back of the car.
- **Dipped headlights** must be switched on at all times, day and night.
- **Speed limits** are 50kph (31mph) in built-up areas, 90kph (55mph) outside built-up areas, 100kph (62mph) on express roads and 130kph (80mph) on motorways.
- According to Poland's **drink-driving law**, the maximum permitted level of alcohol in the bloodstream is 0.02 per cent. If you plan to drive, don't drink alcohol.
- Breakdown assistance is provided by the Polski Związek Motorowy (PZM, www.pzm.pl) which can be reached by calling 9637.

Roads and Tolls
- Poland is currently adding many **new motorways** to replace ageing and over-used single lane express roads.
- **New roads** are being built to European standard though motorways are usually only two-lane. Older single-lane roads are often in very poor condition as are urban streets and roads outside of major cities.

- Traffic jams, roadworks and slow vehicles (old trucks, tractors, horse-drawn carts) slow traffic down to a crawl on many roads.
- **Driving standards** in Poland leave a lot to be desired. Watch out for speeding, dangerous overtaking, erratic behaviour and general disregard for other road users. Drivers are expected to move over for overtaking vehicles.
- Poland has one of the **highest road accident death rates** in the world.
- The new A2 Warsaw-Łódź-Poznań motorway (still under construction) is subject to a **toll**, as are parts of the very efficient Kraków to Wrocłal motorway.
- **Scenic drives** in Poland include the route along the Baltic coast between Gdańsk and the Słowiński National Park as well as many routes through the Tatra, Karkonosze and Beskid Mountains of the south.

Buses

- Poland has a **comprehensive system of inter-city and local buses** operated by regional branches of the former state-run Państwowe Komunikacja Samochodowa (PKS). **Services range from** modern, comfortable, air-conditioned coaches on intercity routes to slow and bouncy local village buses. For **timetables and tickets**, ask at the nearest bus station or tourist office. No national online bus timetable exists as yet.
- A **quicker and more comfortable alternative** to the small PKS branches is Polski Express (www.polskiexpress.pl), which operates between large Polish cities.

Trains

- **Rail services** are operated by Polskie Koleje Państwowe (PKP). Taking the **train is usually quicker** than the bus when travelling between major centres such as Warsaw and Kraków.
- To travel on InterCity and EuroCity services you must have a **seat reservation**.
- **Online timetables** for the entire network are available at www.pkp.com.pl

City Transport in Warsaw

- Warsaw has an incredibly **efficient network** of trams, buses and metro trains operated by ZTM.
- The **main transport hubs** are Centrum metro station and the Warszawa Główny railway station.
- Maps and timetables are displayed at most stops and are available from tourist offices.
- **Tickets** (2.40PLN) can be purchased from ZTM offices and news kiosks.
- **Tickets must be validated** by punching them in machines on board trams and buses and at the entrance to the metro platforms. Those found travelling without a validated ticket will be fined.
- If you intend making multiple journeys in one day, a **24-hour ticket** (7.20PLN) is good value for money.
- The **most useful bus services** are 175 (city centre–airport) and 180 (city centre–Wilanów).

City Transport in Kraków

- Kraków has a **well-run network** of trams and buses operated by MPK.
- The **main transport hub** is Kraków Główny railway station.
- Timetables are displayed at all stops.
- **Tickets** (2.50PLN) can be purchased from news kiosks and ticket machines at stops and on board more modern trams.

- **Tickets must be validated** immediately by punching them in machines on board trams and buses. Those found travelling without a validated ticket will be fined.
- If you intend making multiple journeys in one day, consider purchasing a **24-hour ticket** (10.40PLN).

Taxis
- Every large town and city in Poland has several taxi companies.
- Most taxis are reliable and use meters. Make sure this is switched on at the beginning of the journey.
- Only use taxis with functional meters and with signs on the outside of the vehicle displaying the company name and telephone number.

Accommodation

Poland has a wide range of accommodation to suit all pockets and tastes, especially in tourist hotspots such as Warsaw, Kraków, Gdańsk and Wrocław. Off the beaten track, options are more limited though choice and standards have improved immensely in the last decade. Many new hotels have appeared in the last few years, and the trend continues towards converting historical buildings into attractive places to stay.

Hotels
- These can range from basic hotels with no star rating in small towns through bland business chains in economic hotspots to opulent five-star luxury in the heart of beautifully restored historical centres. The vast majority of hotels have been renovated in the last decade and standards almost brought up to those found in the Western Europe.
- **Boutique hotels** are beginning to appear in Warsaw and Kraków but are few and far between.
- Hotels are **open year-round** and only become booked up in the summer months and around major holidays and religious festivals.
- **Orbis** operates the largest chain in the country (55 hotels); www.orbis.pl

Private Accommodation
- Private accommodation in **houses and cottages** is usually arranged through agencies and tourist offices.
- In smaller towns look out for *noclegi* signs indicating a house owner has rooms to let.
- Make sure private rooms in large cities are **near the city centre** or a convenient tram or bus stop.

Pensions
- These are only **found in the popular tourist areas**, especially in the southern mountainous regions.
- Tourist offices keep lists of guesthouses in their local area.

Agrotourism
- Eco-friendly tourism is **growing fast in Poland** with an ever-increasing number of tour companies offering low-impact holidays in the Tatra and Beskid mountain ranges and the Masurian Lake District.
- Walkers, horse riders, canoeists and cyclists can stay on **owner-operated farms and in cottages** where accommodation comes with organically produced, home-cooked food.

- To book this kind of accommodation yourself, contact local tourist offices in Poland who maintain a list of places to stay approved by the local agro-tourist association; www.ecotourism.org.pl.

Camping

- Poland has more than **270 official campsites**, many of which are equipped with showers, toilets, sports facilities and shops. A further 230 are basic camping grounds with few or no facilities.
- Many campsites have timber cabins for rent.
- The vast majority of campsites are only **open from May to September**.
- Try www.campingo.com for a list of campsites.

Off the Beaten Track

- Hikers in the mountainous regions of Southern Poland often stay in **alpine refuges**. These are usually **run by the Polish Tourist Association (PTTK) or the Polish Mountaineering Association (PZA)** and you can find a **full list** at www.turystyka-gorska.pl/schroniska.php.

Accommodation Prices

The symbols refer to the approximate cost per person per night of a double room in summer and around other major holidays such as Easter and Christmas. Prices drop considerably outside high season and there are very often discounts at weekends. Be aware that around important religious festivals accommodation fills up quickly so check beforehand with the hotel or local tourist office.

€ under 200PLN   €€ 200PLN–500PLN   €€€ over 500PLN

Food and Drink

Polish cuisine is a hot-blooded mix of Jewish, Lithuanian, Hungarian, Ukrainian and Tartar influences, reflecting the country's turbulent history. Though possibly not one of the world's most celebrated cuisines, Polish dishes are some of the tastiest in central and Eastern Europe. Most meals are filling hearty affairs and menus are heavy with meat and dumpling-based dishes, which vary little from region to region.

Eating Out – A Practical Guide

- Many restaurants specialise in **Polish cuisine** though there are now others that serve international staples.
- *Restauracja* is **Polish for restaurant,** *bar mleczny* is a basic self-service cafeteria and *piwnica* is a beer hall. *Karczma* is a tavern or inn where usually only traditional Polish fare is served and a *kawiarnia* is a coffee house.
- **Mealtimes** are around 1–3pm for lunch and 5–7pm for dinner though most restaurants are open all day from around 11am until 11pm.
- **Reservations** are only required at the smartest of eateries.
- Waiting staff don't expect **tips** but if you are satisfied with the service, round the bill up to the nearest 5 or 10 złoty.
- Most restaurants, cafes and pubs open up an outdoor area in the summer

months creating pleasant al fresco dining areas for guests to enjoy on balmy evenings.

■ Although Poles enjoy their meat, vegetarians are relatively well catered for and can usually find meat-free egg, rice, pasta and pancake based dishes on menus.

What to Eat

■ **Starters** include marinated herring, fried mushrooms, goat's cheese, ham, sausage, beef tartare, pork in aspic and potato pancakes.

■ Poland's legendary **soups** are often a filling meal in themselves. The most popular are *żurek* (fermented rye flour soup) and *barszcz* (clear borscht accompanied with a meat filled pastry).

■ *Pierogi* are like crescent-shaped ravioli filled with anything from meat, potato and cottage cheese to mushrooms and sauerkraut, and are usually served with butter.

■ *Naleśniki* **are stuffed pancakes** which come with a range of sweet and savoury fillings.

■ **Fresh fish and seafood** are most common on the Baltic coast and in specialist restaurants in Warsaw and other big cities. Fish (*ryba*) is very often sold by weight with the price per 100g quoted on menus.

■ **Other Polish specialities** you may not have tasted before include *bigos* (meat and sauerkraut stew), *flaki* (tripe), *czernina* (blood soup) and *golonka* (pig knuckle).

■ Popular Polish **snacks** include *zapiekanka* (Polish pizza), pastries and doughnuts.

■ *Kasza gryczana* (buckwheat porridge), *zemniaki* (boiled potatoes), *kapusta* (cabbage), *frytki* (chips) and kluski (dumplings) are common side dishes.

■ **Popular desserts** include *sernik* (cheesecake), *szarlotka* (hot apple cake with ice cream), *lody* (ice cream) and *naleśniki* (pancakes) with sweet toppings.

What to Drink

■ Poland produces some of the **best vodka in the world.** There are hundreds of different brands to choose from and some are flavoured with ingredients such as lemon or honey.

■ **Beer** has become increasingly popular in recent years. Look out for top brands such as Żywiec, Tyskie, Okocim and Lech as well as other locally brewed beers. Half litre glasses often come with a small complimentary bowl of **dripping and bread.**

■ *Woda mineralna* (mineral water) comes either *gazowana* (sparkling) or *niegazowana* (still).

■ **Tea** (*herbata*) is often served in a glass and is drunk without milk. **Coffee** (*kawa*) is all too often instant but filter coffee, latte and cappuccino are becoming increasingly widespread. Turkish coffee is also available on request.

■ Poland produces hardly any **wine** so almost all reds and whites served in restaurants are of foreign origin.

Restaurant Prices
Expect to pay for a three-course meal for one, excluding drinks and service:

€ under 50PLN   €€ 50PLN–100PLN   €€€ over 100PLN

Shopping

Long gone are the days of communist rule when empty shelves and unexciting shops made for a depressing retail experience. Shopping has seen a boom in the last decade with numerous glittering malls and boutique outlets springing up across the country. No single place can claim to be Poland's shopping mecca; all large cities have a wide range of shops, though choice outside major centres is limited.

Practicalities

■ **Most shops are open** from 10 to 6 and Saturday from 10 to 2, large supermarkets may stay open until 10 and there is always at least one general store, which remains open round the clock. Supermarkets are usually open on Sundays but other shops normally stay closed.

■ **Markets** very often finish trading mid-afternoon.

■ **Alcohol** is sold in a separate section of supermarkets and must be paid for immediately.

■ **Credit and debit cards** are now accepted in an ever-increasing number of shops and almost all supermarkets, but most people still prefer cash.

■ Polish shops invariably run out of **change** late in the day, so try to keep small notes and coins just in case.

■ Although the Poles intend to adopt the euro at the earliest opportunity, for the time being the **currency remains the złoty.** However, some shops may already accept euros, though you should never rely on this being the case.

What to Buy

■ **Popular souvenirs** include Baltic amber, local handicrafts and art, antiques, posters and Toruń gingerbread.

■ Many towns and cities have a branch of **Cepelia**, a chain of stores selling a wide range of certified handmade Polish craft items.

■ **Desa** is a countrywide chain of state-owned antique emporia with knowledgeable staff and a wide selection of authentic items on sale. Remember you'll need permission to take anything produced before May 1945 out of the country legally.

■ **Polish vodka** makes a good gift but bear in mind that it may be available in a Polish shop back home (but for double the price).

■ The best place to buy **amber jewellery** is Gdańsk. Always purchase from an established dealer, never from ad hoc street vendors who often sell fake items.

■ Another traditional gift from Gdańsk is **Goldwasser**, a spirit with real pieces of gold leaf swirling around the bottle. The gold is generally considered safe to drink.

■ **EmPik** is a chain of book stores and newagents with branches across the country. This is very often the best place to pick up regional maps, guides, foreign newspapers and even English-language paperbacks.

■ Traditional **handcrafted folk items** such as felt slippers, woollen hats and sheepskin rugs are superb souvenirs from the Tatra Mountains.

■ The Karkonosze Mountains and the area around the border with the Czech Republic is well known for **glass**. Many private workshops and galleries in the region produce and sell unique pieces of decorative glassware and prices are very reasonable.

Entertainment

From top-notch classical music to traditional folk festivals, gripping football matches and relaxing mountain hiking, Poland has entertainment in ample amounts for every visitor. Further details can be obtained from local tourist offices and are listed at the end of the individual chapters in this guide.

Music

■ Poland is one of the best countries in Europe for **classical music and opera**, with every large city boasting several venues. Warsaw, Kraków, Gdańsk and Wrocław are the best places to head to enjoy concerts and performances.
■ The **Sopot International Song Contest** is Poland's biggest annual pop and rock music event with performances by superstar acts from both Eastern and Western Europe.
■ **Jazz** has seen a boom since the collapse of Communism and many jazz clubs and jazz festivals have started up in large cities over the last two decades.
■ **Folk festivals** provide the best opportunities to hear traditional music. Occasionally you may catch live music in restaurants and bars, especially in large cities.

Festivals and Folk Events

■ Every town across Poland holds at least one **festival**, usually in the summer months. Cultural centres such as Kraków and Warsaw have a packed calendar of events with something happening almost every week of the year.
■ The **best places** to catch folk events are Kraków, open-air museums such as Olsztynek and towns and villages in the southern uplands and mountains.
■ As devout Roman Catholics, Poles observe **religious festivals** such as Easter, the Feast of the Assumption (15 August) and a whole host of others with colour and passion.
■ **Pilgrimage** is still a part of Polish life and monasteries such as Jasna Góra in Częstochowa and Licheń are visited by millions of pilgrims annually.

Sport and Outdoor Activities

■ Hiking, climbing, horse riding, skiing and canoeing are all popular activities in the mountainous south.
■ **Swimming** is possible at the height of summer along the Baltic coast where you can also enjoy sandy beaches and endless dunes.
■ **Soccer** is Poland's most popular spectator sport. The top division is called the Orange Ekstraklasa and the season runs from late July through to early May with a two-month winter break in December and January. Matches are played at weekends and tickets are cheap. Teams to look out for are Wisła Kraków, Legia Warszawa and Lech Poznań.
■ Poland's largest **tennis** tournaments are the ATP Tour event in Sopot held in late July and early August and the WTA Tour event in Warsaw, which takes place in May.
■ **Water sports** are particularly popular on the Baltic coast and in the Mazurian Lake District.
■ **Skiing holidays** are becoming increasingly popular in the Tatra Mountains around the winter resort of Zakopane.

Warsaw

Getting Your Bearings

Warsaw (Warszawa) is the nation's capital and the largest city in the country, with 1.7 million inhabitants. It is the political, economic and, to a large extent, the cultural focus of the country and has been since it took on the mantle of capital city from Kraków in 1596.

More than half of Warsaw's population perished and over 80 per cent of its buildings were destroyed during World War II, but the city has risen from the ashes to become a thriving metropolis once again. After the war, some of the historical centre was rebuilt exactly as it had been before, though other quarters were buried under bunker-like reinforced concrete. Warsaw is not exactly Eastern Europe's most attractive capital but it's often the city's turbulent story that fascinates visitors with its many unexpected twists and turns.

The Polish capital can seem confusing to first-timers, but its layout is, in fact, very simple. A grid of thundering motorways makes up the city's heart centred around the Palace of Culture and Science. To the north extends the small Old Town, accessed via Krakowskie Przedmieście, the old royal way, and home to many of the city's tourist sights such as the Royal Castle and the Rynek. To the west of the city centre stand the remnants of Jewish Warsaw and to the east across the River Vistula (Wisła) lies the Praga district.

Previous page:
Cafe terraces
in the Old Town
Square

Left:
Reconstructed
old houses line
Old Town
Square

★ Don't Miss

1 Stare Miasto and Nowe Miasto (Old town and New town) ➤ 42
2 Muranów and Mirów ➤ 44
3 Krakowskie Przedmieście ➤ 46
4 Śródmieście ➤ 48

At Your Leisure

5 Pałac Kultury i Nauki ➤ 50
6 Praga District ➤ 51
7 Park Łazienkowski ➤ 51
8 Wilanów ➤ 51

0 — 500 metres
0 — 500 yards

MOST GDAŃSKI
Z SŁOMIŃSKIEGO
Intraco
STAWKI
K. ANDERSA
MURANOW-SKA
Miedzyparkowa
Bonifraterska
Park im. Traugutta
Wenedow
Konwiktorska
WYBRZEŻE GDAŃSKIE
Sapieżyńska
Zakroczymska
Wołowska
Rajcow
Boleść
WYBRZEŻE HELSKIE 61
Świetojerska
Franciszkańska
Bonifraterska
Rynek Nowego Miasta
Kościelna
Koźla
Freta
Długa
Ogród Zoolog-iczny
Świetojerska
Ogród Krasińskich
Świetojerska
Nowe Miasto
Podwale
Piwna
Piekarska
Rynek Starego Miasta
Ratuszowa
Park Praski
Stare Miasto
 wski Instytut ryczny
Schillera
Miodowa
pl Zamkowy
Zamek Królewski
Grodzka
Zamkowy
Św Cyryla i Metodego
JAGIELLOŃSKA 637
pl Teatralny
Przedmieście
Bednarska
MOST ŚLĄSKO DĄBROWSKI AL SOLIDARNOŚCI
Kościół św Anny
Dobra
pl Wileński
Teatr Wielki
Moliera
Ossolinskich
MARIENSZTAT
Canaletto
Szp Praski
Sierakowskiego
Bazylika Św Floriana
WARSZAWA WILEŃSKA
kowskie mieście 3
Karowa
Karowa
WYBRZEŻE GDAŃSKIE
S Okrzei
S Okrzei
6 Praga
Kościół Św Krzyża
Uniwersytet Warszawski
Obozna
Browarna
WYBRZEŻE KOŚCIUSZKOWSKIE
Dobra
Jagiellonska
Kepna
TARGOWA
Bazar Różyckiego
Nowy Świat
Traugutta
Bibl UW
Barroszewicza
Dynasy
Wisła
Port Praski
K Marcin- kowskiego
Szczecin
Tamka
Topiel
Dobra
Komisariat Rzeczny
Foksal
Kopernika
Gęsczyzna
Tamka
Zajęcza
Solec
WYBRZEŻE SZCZECIŃSKIE 61 801
sokola
WARSZAWA STADION
Most Świetokrzyski
smolna
AL JEROZOLIMSKIE
WARSZAWA POWIŚLE
S Jaracza Ateneum
Muz arodwe
Al 3 Maja
Stadion
AL ZIELENIECKA
Centrum Gieldowe
Al 3 Maja
Książęca
ódmieście
Centralny Park Kultury
Solec
Wioślarska
MOST KS J PONIATOWSKIEGO
usa
Szp Kliniczny nr 1
Ludna
anc rezydenta RP
Rozbrat
Czerniakowska
Okrąg
ul Wilanowska
WYBRZEŻE SZCZECIŃSKIE
WAŁ MIEDZESYŃSKI
Sejm Senat RP
Śniegockiej
Kpt K M Krska
Płyta Desantu
Gomulassa
Śniegockiej
SOLEC 7
Rozbrat
Fabryczna
61
Kminska
Warszawa Towarzystwo Wioślarskie
AL ARMII LUDOWEJ
Łazienkowska
E30 2
Torwar
MOST ŁAZIENKOWSKI
J Kusocinskiego
CWKS Legia
8 Wilanów

In Two Days

If you're not quite sure where to begin your travels, this itinerary recommends a practical and enjoyable two days in Warsaw, taking in some of the best places to see using the Getting Your Bearings map on the previous page. For more information see the main entries.

Day One

Morning
Start your day with coffee and Polish doughnuts at a café on **3 Krakowskie Przedmieście** (left, ➤ 46–47) while students from the nearby university hurry, books in hand, to lectures. Spend the next hour strolling north along the Royal Way, admiring the churches and palaces as you go. This will bring you to the Royal Castle (opposite, **1** ➤ 42–43), where a tour should finish just in time for lunch.

Lunch
What better place to do lunch than beneath a sunshade at one of the restaurants on the Rynek Starego Miasta (**1** ➤ 43) as you watch tourists from all over the world file past and admire the restored architecture of Warsaw's most celebrated piazza. After lunch, continue along ul. Freta to the Barbakan and the New Town (**1** ➤ 43).

Afternoon and Evening
Take in a couple of the city-centre museums and galleries **4** before heading to the **5 Palace of Culture and Science** (➤ 50), where the high-speed lift will whizz you skywards to the lofty viewing platform. End the day with some filling Polish fare at a local restaurant such as Delicja Polska (➤ 54) or the communist theme restaurant, Oberża Pod Czerwonym Wieprzem (➤ 54).

Day Two

Morning
The first task of the day is to buy a 24-hour public transport

ticket (available from most news kiosks) as today you are going to discover the suburbs and city limits. Your first destination is **6 Praga** (➤ 51) and the Russian Bazaar (take any tram heading east from the city centre) for a spot of shopping. From there, hop on tram 21 or 25 to Al. Solidarności which cuts through the Praga District, home to Warsaw Zoo, the attractive Russian Church of SS Cyril and Methodius and the Church of SS Michael and Florian.

Lunch
For a fabulous lunch take tram 7 or 13 to the terminus, where you'll find Fabrika Trzciny (➤ 54), one of the best restaurants in the city. Make sure you order a filling dish as you've still got a lot of travelling to do.

Afternoon
Head back to the centre to catch bus 180 to **8 Wilanów** (➤ 51), where you can spend the afternoon admiring the exquisite interiors of the palace and strolling the gardens. Board the same bus heading north to reach **7 Łazienki Park** (➤ 51), your last stop.

Evening
After a relaxing walk around the park, dine in style at the Belvedere restaurant (➤ 53) in the New Orangery. Finish the day with a classical music concert or theatre performance at the Island Amphitheatre.

❶ Stare Miasto and Nowe Miasto

You might assume the tall town houses and churches that line the cobbled streets and squares of the Old and New Towns have stood here for centuries but you would be wrong. After the fighting that took place in Warsaw during World War II, all that remained of this area of the city was a smouldering pile of rubble and almost everything you see today was rebuilt in the 1950s and 1960s. The Old Town was listed as a UNESCO World Heritage Site in 1980, just reward for the work of the skilful Polish restorers.

Royal Castle

One of the highlights of any visit to Warsaw is a tour of the pink building of the Royal Castle (Zamek Królewski), on Plac Zamkowy. A royal residence appeared here in the 14th century but it wasn't until the reign of King Stanisław August Poniatowski that it was transformed into a grand baroque affair and one of the most lavish palaces in Europe. It stayed that way until 1945, when Hitler issued an order for the retreating Nazis to blow it up. Rebuilding work financed entirely by donations from abroad only began in 1971 and it took restorers 13 years to re-create the historical structure. The most striking room must be the Great Assembly Hall, with its gilt stucco work, chandeliers and frescoed ceiling.

Rynek Starego Miasta

A short walk along ul. Świętojańska will bring you to Warsaw's historical showpiece, the Old Town Square. Restored three- to six-floor burghers' houses line every flank and gaze down on Warsaw's most famous and most photographed landmark, the **Mermaid Statue**, dating from 1855. The square is always a hive of activity, with horse-drawn carriage drivers offering tours, waiters scurrying through the forest of café tables that invades the cobbles in summer, tourists taking photographs and buskers and instant portrait painters trying to attract the attention of passers-by. The parade of restaurants, cafés and souvenir shops is interrupted on the northern side by the **Warsaw History Museum**, which tells the story of the city from its origins to the restoration of the post-war years.

New Town

The so-called New Town lies immediately to the north of the Rynek along ul. Nowomiejski. The main attractions here are the **Maria Skłodowska-Curie Museum** occupying the house she once used to, and the Rynek Nowego Miasta (New Town Square), an altogether quieter affair than its neighbour.

TAKING A BREAK

On Old Town Square you'll be spoiled for choice for places to stop. With so many tourists around, prices here couldn't be described as "Polish", but you are paying for the location. Some offer very reasonable lunch menus for 15–20PLN.

Horses and carriages await passengers in Old Town Square

➕ 199 D4

Royal Castle (Zamek Królewski)
✉ Plac Zamkowy 4 ☎ 022 355 5170; www.zamek-krolewski.pl
🕐 Daily 11–6 💲 Moderate

Warsaw History Museum (Muzeum Historyczne M.St. Warszawy)
✉ Rynek Starego Miasta 28 ☎ 022 635 1625; www.mhw.pl 🕐 Tue–Sun 10:30–3:30 (Tue, Thu until 6) 💲 Moderate

Maria Skłodowska-Curie Museum
✉ ul. Freta 16 ☎ 022 831 8092 🕐 Tue–Sun 9:30–4 💲 Moderate

STARE MIASTO AND NOWE MIASTO: INSIDE INFO

In more depth The Old Town is flanked to the west by sturdy red-brick defensive walls which begin at Plac Zamkowy and end just beyond the Barbakan, a 16th-century tower where musicians often perform for the tourists and artists sell their wares. On summer evenings join the Poles for a pleasant stroll along the fortifications, which are being restored brick by brick.

2 Muranów and Mirów

What remains of Warsaw's Jewish heritage is scattered around the districts of Mirów and Muranów to the north and west of the centre. Once home to a Jewish community that numbered almost 400,000 before World War II, this was the location of the horrific ghetto created by the Nazis in 1940 and obliterated by them when quelling the uprising which broke out there in 1943. Very little and very few survived.

Exploring the area on foot can be an exhausting but rewarding and emotional experience. Start in ul. Stawki at the **Umschlagplatz** where Jews would be loaded into cattle trucks for the journey to the death camps, now marked by an unexceptional marble monument. Some 15 minutes' walk southwest is the Jewish cemetery which, somewhat surprisingly, came through the war intact and which contains more than 150,000 Jewish gravestones, the largest number anywhere in Europe.

Back on ul. Stawki your next stop should be **Willy Brandt Square**, named after the former German chancellor who fell to his knees here during an official visit in 1970 in an act of atonement for Nazi war crimes. Here also is the granite **Monument to the Heroes of the Ghetto**, in the Socialist

Monument to the Heroes of the Ghetto

JEWISH HERITAGE: INSIDE INFO

In more depth Finally it looks as though Warsaw is to get the **Jewish museum** many think it lacks and deserves. An ultra-modern multimedia facility tracing a millennium of Jewish history in Poland is set to open in the city centre before the end of the decade. To keep track of the new museum's progress, check out the website at www.jewishmuseum.org.pl.

Realist style, made from stone that the Nazis had brought to Warsaw for their victory monument.

A more shocking experience is provided by a tour of the **Pawiak Prison** at ul. Dzielna 24, which witnessed the execution of around 37,000 prisoners by the Gestapo. Remnants of everyday life in the Jewish community can be seen at the **Nożyk Synagogue**, which incredibly saw out World War II, and nearby ul. Próżna is a single ghostly pre-war street whose derelict buildings are still pockmarked with bullet holes. Two fragments of the wall that once surrounded the ghetto have been left standing between ul. Sienna 55 and ul. Złota 62 and in ul. Waliców.

The only major Jewish site outside the old Jewish quarter is the **Jewish Historical Institute** (Żydowski Instytut Historyczny), founded in 1994 on the other side of the city centre. It has exhibitions on many aspects of Jewish life, Jews across Poland and the Warsaw ghetto.

The Nożyk Synagogue was founded in 1900 by a wealthy local family

TAKING A BREAK

The Jewish sights are slightly off the beaten track and there are few places to rest aching feet and take on refreshments. **The Barista** at Złota 59 is decent coffee stop while **Folk Gospoda** at ul. Waliców 13 serves filling Polish fare. **Oberża Pod Czerwonym Wieprzem** at ul. Żelazna 68 (► 54) is a communist theme restaurant.

✚ 198 B5 (Muranów), 198 A4 (Mirów)

Pawiak Prison
✚ 198 B4 ✉ ul. Dzielna 24/26 ☎ 022 831 9289 🕐 Wed–Sun 10–4
💲 Free

Jewish Historical Institute
✚ 198 C4 ✉ ul. Tłomackie 3/5 ☎ 022 827 9221; www.jewishinstitute.org.pl
🕐 Mon–Fri 9–4 💲 Moderate

❸ Krakowskie Przedmieście

Long, wide and proud Krakowskie Przedmieście is the beginning of the route Polish kings would take between the Royal Castle in the Old Town and their summer residence at Łazienki Palace. Sometimes called the Royal Way, this most historical and grand of Warsaw boulevards is lined with palaces, churches, university buildings, hotels and restaurants, and is always busy with ambling tourists and students hurrying to lectures. It's the most scenic way of reaching the Old Town from the centre and has just received a multi-million złoty facelift.

Heading from the city centre, the first buildings of note you see on the left belong to the **university** and incorporate the baroque **Kościół św Krzyża** (Church of the Holy Cross), which was completely destroyed in 1944, though you'd never guess it today. Opposite the university sits a statue of **Copernicus** holding his heliocentric model. Continue north past more university buildings to the **Pałac Czapskich** (Czapski Palace, left) an erstwhile home to Frederyk Chopin and currently the Polish Academy of Fine Arts. Some 100m (91 yards) further on the right stands the beautiful baroque **Kościół Sióstr Wizytek** (Church of the Nuns of the Visitation), set back from the road and shrouded by tall trees. It is one of the very few historical buildings to survive World War II without a

KRAKOWSKIE PRZEDMIEŚCIE: INSIDE INFO

Hidden gem Classical music fans will be fascinated to learn that the Church of the Holy Cross houses an urn containing Chopin's heart. It was removed on the composer's request as he feared being buried alive. His sister brought it back to Warsaw from Paris (where he died) and placed it in an urn in the church which has almost become a place of pilgrimage for admirers of Poland's greatest musical figure.

Above: The presidential palace has witnessed several key events in Poland's history

Left: The Copernicus Monument

scratch and boasts an original lavishly decorated interior.

Across a small park from the church rises one of the best-known buildings in the capital, the majestic neo-Renaissance **Bristol Hotel**, dating from 1901, Warsaw's top place to stay. Guests at the Bristol enjoy the loftiest of neighbours as none other than the Polish president resides next door in the **Pałac Radziwiłłów** (Radziwiłł Palace). This Polish Buckingham Palace (there is a faint similarity) and its forerunner witnessed some of the most important events in Polish history such as the signing of the May Third Constitution in 1791, the signing of the Warsaw Pact in 1955 and talks between the communists and Solidarity in 1989. The now heavily guarded and gated palace only became a residence for the head of state when Lech Wałęsa decided the Belweder in Łazienki Park was cramping his style.

Some 100m (91 yards) further along your next stop should be at the 1889 **Mickiewicz monument** which stands in a small park on the right. The 17th-century **Kościół Karmelitów** (Carmelite Church) rises just behind. From there it's a short walk to the impressive baroque **Kościół św Anny** (Church of St Anne) with its huge white columns and almost freestanding belfry, which can be climbed for a small charge. Your final stop is in front of the Royal Castle on the steps surrounding the **statue of King Sigismund III**, the monarch responsible for moving the capital from Kraków to Warsaw in 1596.

TAKING A BREAK

Midway through a leisurely stroll along the length of Krakowskie Przedmieście, why not treat yourself and stop off at the Viennese-style **Cafe Bristol** inside the Bristol Hotel for an upper-crust coffee accompanied by pastries baked on the premises? For something slightly less distressing for the wallet, try **Batida (No 13)** on the corner immediately opposite which serves a wide range of syrupy, sugary Polish treats and coffee any way you like it.

4 Śródmieście

Warsaw's Śródmieście or city centre is roughly the area
defined by the River Vistula, the former Jewish quarters and
the Old Town in the north. Although this is certainly not
the most attractive part of the city, there are some islands
of history and greenery to be enjoyed in what otherwise can
seem like an endless sea of thundering dual carriageways,
dank underpasses and soot-streaked concrete.

Museums

You should allow at least half a day to visit the **Polish
National Museum** (Muzeum Narodowe), which houses a fine
collection of Egyptian, Greek and Roman artefacts and a huge
array of Polish, Italian, Flemish and German art from the 15th
to the 20th century. The museum is as good a place as any to
become acquainted with a few of the stars of Polish painting,
namely Wyspiański, Malczewski and Matejko.

The wide-ranging collection of art in the **Muzeum Kolekcji
im. Jana Pawła II** was donated to the Catholic Church in
1986 by the Carroll-Porczyński family. The walls display a
real mixed bag and the exhibition is rather oddly displayed
according to theme not period, but it's still worth an hour or
two of perusal.

Slightly outside the Śródmieście, the new focus for World
War II history in Warsaw is the impressive **Uprising Museum**
which opened in 2004 to mark the 60th
anniversary of the historical events which
took place here. The museum has a somewhat
chaotic layout by design, perhaps to give an
impression of the confusing and frenzied way
events during the uprising unfolded and this
works well alongside the period uniforms,
weapons, photographs, documents and mock-
ups of sewers and bunkers to relate the story
of the 63-day uprising against the Nazis in
1944. Be sure not to miss the film shown
in English.

**An exhibit
within the
Uprising
Museum**

Gardens

The largest formal gardens in the city centre
are the **Saxon Gardens** (Ogród Saski),
a welcome stretch of green etched with
pathways and dotted with benches, baroque
statues and mature trees. This ranks as one of
oldest public parks in the world, having been
laid out in 1727, and on warm days it still
attracts hundreds of picnickers, dog walkers
and joggers. Until 1944 it was also home to
the royal palace, blown up by the Nazis and
never rebuilt (though plans were drawn up).

The fountain in the heart of the Saxon Gardens dates from 1855

TAKING A BREAK

An interesting place to escape the city is the arty **Cafe Kulturalna** (opposite the theatre within the Palace of Culture and Science), which retains a highbrow pre-theatre atmosphere (though it can get a bit smoky). Alternatively, for a spot of lunch try the **Bistro Trojka** (opposite the high-speed lift ticket office in the main building), a much less hazy but blander affair. Other places to head for a latte fix include **Wayne's Coffee** (Al. Jerozolimskie 56c) and **Green Coffee** (ul. Maszałkowska 84).

➕ 198 C2

National Museum
➕ 198 C2 ✉ Al. Jerozolimskie 3 ☎ 022 621 1031; www.mnw.art.pl
🕐 Tue–Fri 10–4, Sat, Sun 10–6 💰 Moderate

Muzeum Kolekcji im. Jana Pawła II
➕ 198 C4 ✉ Plac Bankowy 1 ☎ 022 620 2725; www.muzeummalarstwa.pl
🕐 Daily 10–5 (shorter hours in winter) 💰 Moderate

Uprising Museum
➕ 198 A4 ✉ ul. Grzybowska 79 ☎ 022 539 79 05; www.1944.pl 🕐 Mon–Fri
8–6, Sat–Sun 10–6 🚊 Trams 20, 22, 24, 32, 45 💰 Inexpensive

ŚRÓDMIEŚCIE: INSIDE INFO

Hidden "gem" There's no denying that central Warsaw is a bit of a carbuncle and no other place typifies the urban planning crimes committed on the city post war better than the **main railway station**. Built in the 1970s, the building is due a facelift sometime soon but until then will remain a dreary monument to communist-era architecture. Sadly, visitors' all-important first impressions of Warsaw are often formed in its reinforced concrete bowels as they attempt to battle their way out of a labyrinth of underpasses and tunnels to street level.

At Your Leisure

Palace of Culture and Science illuminated at night

⑤ Pałac Kultury i Nauki

Gift from Stalin to the Polish people, towering symbol of 40 years of communist rule, exquisite example of socialist realism, tourist attraction, or eyesore occupying a prime piece of real estate in central Warsaw, the Stalinist-era Palace of Culture and Science is as controversial today as it has ever been and every Varsovian has his or her opinion on it. Built between 1952 and 1955, at 231m (758 feet) it is still Poland's tallest building despite the shiny new skyscrapers that have sprouted up all around it. The architectural design is an almost exact copy of the Seven Sisters towers that line Moscow's outer ring road, and the ornate Stalinist interior contains more than 3,000 rooms, acres of office space, cinemas, museums, three theatres and a huge congress centre, which has hosted events as diverse as Communist party conferences and the Miss World competition. The main attraction for tourists is the viewing platform 114m (374 feet) up, affording truly spectacular views of the Warsaw cityscape. The platform is reached by high-speed lift from the ground floor where there are a couple of restaurants.

➕ 198 B3 ✉ Plac Defilad 1 ☎ 022 656 7600; www.pkin.pl ⏰ Daily 9–8 💲 Expensive

Church of Saints Cyril and Methodius

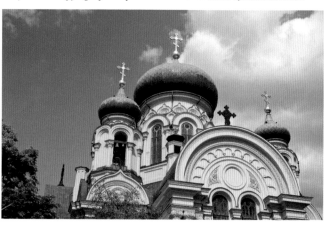

The gardens at Wilanów

Nearby the king had an **amphitheatre** built on a small island where performances with a watery theme take place in the summer months. Other places of interest in the park include the **Chopin Monument** and various other small palaces, including the **White House** (Biały Dom) built in 1777 for the king's favourite mistress, and the **Belweder**, residence for Polish heads of state from World War I until 1995.

🔲 198 B1 Bul. Agrykola 1 ⏰ Dawn–dusk
📷 180 💷 Free

Łazienki Palace

🔲 198 C1 ☎ 022 506 0167; www.lazienki-krolewskie.pl ⏰ Tue–Sun 9–4 💷 Expensive

❽ Praga District

The Praga District, on the right bank of the Vistula, suffered only minor damage during World War II and gives at least some impression of how pre-1945 Warsaw might have looked. The principal draw on this side of the river is the **Russian Market**, which wraps itself around the almost unpronounceable Dziesięciolecia Stadium (➤ 55). Two impressive churches grace the district: the **Eastern Orthodox Church of SS Cyril and Methodius**, with its onion domes and ochre façades, and the neo-Gothic **Church of SS Michael and Florian** can both be found on Al. Solidarności, which crosses the river on its way from the city centre. The only other attraction is **Warsaw Zoo,** which occupies 40ha (99 acres) of the large Park Praski on the banks of the Vistula and is a great place to bring the children.

🔲 199 E3

Zoo

🔲 199 E4 ✉ ul. Ratuszowa 1/3 ☎022 619 4041; www.zoo.waw.pl ⏰ Daily 9–7 📷 Trams 4, 13, 23, 26, 32, 46 💷 Moderate

❼ Park Łazienkowski

This area of verdant parkland 4km (2.5 miles) south of the city centre once served as the summer retreat for Polish King Stanisław August Poniatowski who had a palace, lake and various follies constructed here in the late 1770s. The highlight of the Łazienki Park must be the **Łazienki Palace** (Pałac Łazienkowski), the former royal residence designed by Italian architect Domenico Merlini, which looks as though it's floating on the man-made lake. Join a guided tour to view its noble interiors.

❽ Wilanów

The perfect antidote to Warsaw's boxy city centre is the palace and gardens at Wilanów on the southern outskirts, often described as the "Polish Versailles". Built in the late 17th century by King Jan Sobieski and added to by later monarchs, this is Warsaw's most majestic baroque palace and the guided tour plus a stroll in the adjacent gardens makes a relaxing half-day excursion.

🔲 199 D1 (off map) ✉ Bul. S K Potockiego 10/16 ☎ 022 842 8101; www.wilanow-palac.art.pl ⏰ Mon, Wed, Sat 9:30–6:30; Tue, Thu, Fri 9:30–4:30; Sun 10:30–6:30 📷 116, 180 💷 Moderate; Sun free

Chopin Monument in Łazienki Park

Where to... Stay

Prices

Expect to pay per night for a double room (in peak season):

€ under 200PLN   €€ 200PLN–500PLN   €€€ over 500PLN

Bristol €€€

Widely acclaimed as Warsaw's top place to stay, the Bristol is an unforgettable place to stay. Built at the turn of the 20th century, it was an emblem of the city's aspirations to be regarded as a world-class metropolis. All rooms are individually designed and, throughout, you will be impressed by the imperially high ceilings, dazzling chandeliers and immaculate art nouveau decor. With its location on Warsaw's most illustrious thoroughfare, a long list of facilities and services and an opulent ambience, there's no better place in the capital.

🚩 198 C3 ✉ Krakowskie Przedmieście 42/44 ☎ 022 551 1000; www.warsaw.lemeridien.com

Oki Doki €

Though officially backpacker accommodation, this extremely well-run hostel-cum-hotel in the heart of the city centre would put many a mainstream Polish hotel to shame. It has been voted one of the top ten hostels in the world, and with its superb and or iginally designed facilities, very helpful staff and comfortable guest rooms, it isn't hard to see why. If slumming it in a dorm is not your style, go for an arty double or single. There's

a more upmarket branch directly opposite the Royal Castle.

🚩 198 C3 ✉ Plac Dąbrowskiego 3 ☎ 022 826 5112; www.okidoki.pl

Praski €€

Why not see Warsaw from a different angle and stay in the up-and-coming Praga district on the right bank of the Vistula? The renovated Praski may sport only two stars but punches way above its weight. Rooms are clean and comfortable, staff are welcoming and trams leave from almost outside the main door to whisk you into the thick of the tourist action on the other side of the river. Considerable weekend discounts.

🚩 199 E3 ✉ Al. Solidarności 61 ☎ 022 201 6300; www.praski.pl

Rialto €€€

Poland's first boutique hotel, in the city's business district south of the main railway station takes its art seriously and it's claimed that the owners scoured emporia

across Europe to stock its rooms and corridors with genuine art deco treasures. Each room has been individually designed and the attention to detail is incredible. One room will take you back to swish 1920s New York, another to early 20th-century Vienna and yet another to colonial Africa. The chic art deco theme continues in the hotel restaurant.

🚩 198 B2 ✉ ul. Wilcza 73 ☎ 022 584 8700; www.rialto.pl

Le Regina €€€

Occupying a restored 18th-century palace just a few hundred metres north of the Rynek Starego Miasta, this exquisite five-star boutique hotel is possibly Warsaw's most romantic and certainly one of the city's most comfortable. The 61 rooms are tastefully furnished, there's an award-winning restaurant and the indoor swimming pool is the cherry on the cake.

🚩 199 D4 ✉ Kościelna 12 ☎ 022 531 6000; www.leregina.com

Where to...
Eat and Drink

Prices

Expect to pay for a three-course meal for one, excluding drinks:
€ under 50PLN €€ 50PLN–100PLN €€€ over 100PLN

Babooshka €

Tucked away in a modern complex just off Krakowskie Przedmieście, this intimate eatery serves up a mix of cheap and filling Russian, Belorussian and Ukrainian fare such as *vareniki* (sweet ravioli), *bliny* (pancakes) and *pelmeny* (savoury ravioli) which diners can happily wash down with Kiev's finest Obolon beer. The diminutive dining room with its Ukrainian ceremonial towels, gleaming samovars and chunky timber benches makes you feel as though you are eating in someone's front room in Siberia, all intentional of course as this is not your typical over-priced exclusive Russian restaurant.

🚹 199 D3 ✉ ul. Oboźna 9 ☎ 022 406 3366 🕐 Daily 10–10

Bar Mleczny Pod Barbakanem €

Eat out communist-era style at this typical self-service cafeteria, a miraculous survivor of the last 20 years of social change, and a Polish institution. For those not in the know, a milk bar serves inexpensive Polish food in a no-frills environment. All dishes have to be ordered and picked up at one counter and paid up at a serving hatch. Menus are posted on large boards and you'll need at least some Polish to be able to request what you fancy. Good for a cheap and cheerful lunch, less apt for a romantic dinner for two, Pod Barbakanem is an unexpected find in the increasingly gentrified Old Town.

🚹 199 D4 ✉ ul. Mostowa 27/29 ☎ 022 831 4737 🕐 Mon–Fri 8am–5pm, Sat–Sun 9am–5pm

Belvedere €€€

Upmarket service and top-notch victuals in the sumptuous surroundings of the elegant New Orangery, in popular Łazienki Park, make dining here a memorable experience. The menu features gourmet takes on Polish peasant fare containing some unexpected ingredients. The lean portions of exceptionally composed food are a welcome change from Poland's many rural theme taverns.

🚹 198 B1 ✉ New Orangery, Łazienki Park ☎ 022 841 2250 🕐 Daily noon–11pm

BrowArmia €€

Warsaw's first microbrewery restaurant is too sleek to generate a really raucous Munich-style beer hall atmosphere, but this is more than compensated by the superb dark, wheat and light lager beers that help to wash down hearty helpings of duck with apple, steak, pork knuckle and schnitzel. This is actually located on Krakowskie Przedmieście despite its official address.

🚹 198 C3 ✉ ul. Królewska 1 ☎ 022 826 5455 🕐 Daily noon–midnight

Ceprownia €

A folksy little piece of the Tatra Mountains in central Warsaw, this tiny theme restaurant on the city's main historical thoroughfare is bedecked with spinning wheels, dolls in national costume and other knick-knacks with a Carpathian theme. The hearty shepherd's menu is meat-heavy and many of the meals include sheeps cheese, so typical of Poland's southern alpine reaches. Popular with students from the nearby university. Bus 175 stops almost outside the door.

🏠 198 C3 ☒ ul. Krakowskie Przedmieście 7 ☎ 022 828 2884 🕐 Daily 10am–midnight

Chłopskie Jadło €€

One of two Warsaw branches of this famous nationwide chain, where diners munch on giant portions of hearty country fare among strings of garlic, chunky agricultural implements, kitchen utensils and other rural regalia. The veal and wild mushrooms in cream and white wine sauce is not to be missed, the soups are meals in themselves and you're unlikely to have room for a dessert such as pancakes filled with cottage cheese and vanilla sauce. Very popular with weekending Polish families.

🏠 198 B2 ☒ Plac Konstytucji 1 ☎ 022 339 1717 🕐 Daily noon–midnight

Deco Kredens €€

The newest of three eateries making up the Kredens group, this café is decked out in art deco wrought iron, stained glass and oversize sepia images in an attempt to re-create interwar Bohemia. You can decide whether it works or not as you sample well-prepared Italo-Polish cooking or just sip a coffee.

🏠 198 C3 ☒ ul. Ordynacka 13 ☎ 022 826 0660 🕐 Daily noon–11

Delicja Polska €€

Despite the modern exterior, inside this place is as chintzy as Polish restaurants come with flowery wallpaper, tables laden with crystal and fresh blooms, still-life oils adorning the walls and old-fashioned service. The menu is an inspired blend of Polish and international cuisine.

🏠 198 B2 ☒ ul. Koszykowa 54 ☎ 022 630 8850 🕐 Daily 11am–midnight

Fabrika Trzciny €€

Housed in a former sugar refinery dating from 1916, this superb modern eatery deep in the Praga district has a clean-cut exposed brick and glass interior, an imaginative menu of Polish classics and international favourites and impeccable service. The building is also home to an art gallery, a well-known trendy nightclub, a conference hall and a theatre space, and is well worth the trip out from the city centre.

🏠 Off map 199 F3 ☒ ul. Otwocka 14 ☎ 022 619 1705 🕐 Tue–Sun noon–11pm

Oberża Pod Czerwonym Wieprzem €€

The "Inn Below the Red Hog" is Warsaw's only real communist theme restaurant but is a cut above those found in other former Eastern Bloc cities. The spartan timber interior, red flags, socialist anthems on the CD player and waiting staff dressed in the uniforms of the erstwhile communist youth movement are the backdrop to an unforgettable experience. The socialist theme even spreads to the menu featuring dishes with titles such as "Proletarian Pork Chop", "First Secretary's Catfish" and many others that you would need a degree in Eastern European history to comprehend.

🏠 198 A3 ☒ ul. Żelazna 68 ☎ 022 850 3144 🕐 Daily 11am–midnight

Polka €€

The latest creation by restaurateur Magda Gessler, a leading light of the Warsaw gastronomic scene, is a striking place to eat, the eight dining rooms each decorated with different traditional rural motifs inspiring guests to tuck into the equally rustic menu. Unlike other rural theme restaurants, this one is carried off with style and is one of the treats of the capital's dining scene – and you won't have to break the bank to partake.

🏠 199 D4 ☒ ul. Świętojańska 2 ☎ 022 635 3535 🕐 Daily noon–11

Where to...Shop

Russian Bazaar

Warsaw's infamous Russian bazaar, the largest outdoor market in Europe, comes alive every morning around the disused Dziesięciolecia Stadium on the right bank of the Vistula. The stadium was built in the 1950s to celebrate ten years of communism in Poland but was abandoned in the late 1980s, after which it was invaded by Russians selling off Red Army surplus including, it is rumoured, guns and other military hardware. In the intervening years the Russians have given way to Vietnamese traders, and Soviet pin badges and *matrioshka* dolls have been replaced by imitation Levis and Chinese bras. Still a sight to behold, this huge market is actually slated for closure as the stadium is set to be revived for the 2012

European football championships. Go and explore it now before this post-communist phenomenon disappears under glass and steel.

Flea Market

Held Saturday and Sunday mornings in the western district of Koło, the famous **Bazar na Kole** (literally "Market in Koło") provides an opportunity to peruse antiques and bric-a-brac stalls offering anything from World War II medals and Socialist-era LPs to kitsch oil paintings and pre-war silverware. This market is a few notches more upmarket than the Russian Bazaar though you're no longer likely to unearth any precious treasure here. The market opens around 7am and is all over by mid-afternoon. Haggling is expected so never pay the first price quoted.

Polish Handicrafts

Cepelia is a nationwide chain of outlets selling genuine Polish art and handicrafts. Any item bearing the Cepelia trademark is guaranteed to have been made by hand in Poland (as opposed to a machine in Shanghai) which makes Cepelia stores the best places to pick up Polish ceramics, wickerwork, jewellery, furniture, embroidery, lace and a whole host of other traditionally produced articles, which make superb souvenirs. There are branches in Warsaw at ul. Marszałkowska 99/101, Pl. Konstytucji 5 and several other locations around the city.

Antiques

Desa is another state-owned nationwide chain of stores, this time specialising in antiques. Inside these emporia you will discover all kinds of items from antique furniture to porcelain services, art deco jewellery to Swiss watches and staff who know their stuff. Warsaw

branches at Ul. Marszałkowska 34/50 and Rynek Starego Miasta 4/6 are worth a browse, even if you don't intend buying anything. Be aware that permission is required if you want to export items produced before 1945.

Posters

Poster art is a Polish speciality and one of the best places to view and buy is **Galeria Plakatu** at Rynek Starego Miasta 23 which stocks authentic film, theatre, circus, political and reprint pre-World War II posters. Solidarity posters from the 1980s are particularly popular.

Shopping Malls

As capital city, Warsaw probably offers the best mall shopping experience in Poland. If you've come to Poland to flex the plastic, make a beeline for **Galeria Centrum** (ul Marszałkowska), **Sadyba Best Mall** (ul Powsińska) and **Blue City** (Al. Jerozolimskie 179) but don't expect bargains.

Where To...
Be Entertained

OPERA

The **Great Theatre** on Plac Teatralny plays host to the National Opera (Teatr Wielki-Opera Narodowa) and is the number one venue for Polish opera performances as well as more familiar favourites. For programmes and tickets visit www.teatrwielki.pl or tel: 022 826 3288.

CINEMA

Kinoteka in the Palace of Culture and Science is arguably most interesting picture house in the city. Check the programme and buy tickets online at www.kinoteka.pl or tel: 022 551 7070. Before booking, make ure the film you want to see has not been dubbed into Polish. Other cinemas in the city centre include **Luna** (Marszalkowska 28; www.kinoluna.pl), **Silver Screen** (ul. Puławska 17; www.silverscreen.com.pl) ar d **Multikino Złote Tarasy** (ul Złota 59; www.multikino.pl).

CLASSICAL MUSIC

The **Filharmonia** (ul. Jasna 5, tel: 022 551 7128; www.filharmonia. pl) is Warsaw's top classical music venue and base for the Warsaw Philharmonic Orchestra. A wide range of concerts is performed here by the Philharmonic Orchestra and visiting bodies. Unfortunately everybody at the Filharmonia takes a long but well-deserved break in the summer months.

The **Fryderyk Chopin Society** (Towarzystwo im. Fryderyka Chopina) organises piano concerts at many venues throughout Warsaw including free Sunday recitals in Łazienki Park and at Żelazowa Wola (Chopin's birthplace just outside Warsaw). See the society website at www.tifc.chopin.pl for details. The **International Chopin Festival** takes place annually in the second half of August and is normally made up of around 20 concerts which take place at the Filharmonia and a handful of other venues. The event is a must for anyone who regards themselves a fan, so for more info, log onto www.infochopin.pl.

For a break from Chopin, why not try the **Warsaw Chamber Opera** (www.operakameralna. pl) who hold an annual Mozart Festival in June and July. Warsaw's premier jazz hangout is **Tygmont** (ul. Mazowiecka 6/8; www.tygmont. com.pl), which has been listed as one of the 100 best jazz clubs in the world. Sessions usually start at around 8pm and can go on until the early hours.

WHAT'S ON

In Your Pocket Guide (six times yearly), **Warsaw Insider** (monthly) and *The Warsaw Voice* (weekly) are all good English-language publications providing information on forthcoming events in the city as well as restaurant, bar, club and cafe listings and a lot more besides. Warsaw's **tourist offices** are also rich sources of information for entertainment options.

ONLINE TICKET SALES

To buy tickets over the internet for any event taking place in the capital before you even leave home, try www.bilecik.info, www.ticketonline. pl or www.ticketpro.pl.

The Northeast

Getting Your Bearings

Northeast Poland, bordering on the Kaliningrad Enclave,
Lithuania and Belarus, consists of the four historical regions
of Warmia and Masuria in the north and Mazovia (around
Warsaw) and Podlasie in the south.

Bison in
Białowieski

Previous page:
The cathedral
tower at Płock

★ Don't Miss

At Your Leisure

While Warmia and Masuria form a tranquil region of forests and lakes, Mazovia contains Poland's largest cities (Warsaw and Łódż) and the mighty River Vistula. Podlasie is a forested plain stretching to the Belarusian border and boasting the Białowieski National Park, one of the country's most popular attractions. Very often, travelling in the less frequented northeast takes you firmly off the beaten track and the region is the perfect place to experience authentic country life and rural ways.

Although less visited than other more illustrious parts of the country, this quartet of regions possesses some of the most distinctive places of interest Poland has to offer. The Elbląg–Ostróda Canal in Warmia is a unique technical wonder and a trip between the two towns manages to be both fascinating and relaxing at the same time. The Białowieża National Park is also unique in containing the last European bison in the wild, and Lake niardy is the country's biggest and a Mecca for water sports fans. The northeast also boasts one of the finest outdoor museums in the country, which can be found on the edge of the small town of Olsztynek.

**Olsztyn's
Gothic castle**

In Four Days

If you're not quite sure where to begin your travels, this itinerary
recommends a practical and enjoyable four days in Northeast
Poland, taking in some of the best places to see using the Getting
Your Bearings map on the previous page. For more information see
the main entries.

Day One

Morning
Make an early start in Elbląg to board a cruise bound for Ostróda via
the slipways and serene lakes of the **1 Kanal Ostródsko–Elbląski** (above,
► 62–63). Spend the day relaxing, watching wildlife and observing the
extraordinary method the canal uses to transport boats up and down hills.

Evening
Either stay the night in Ostróda or make your way to **2 Olsztyn** (► 64–65),
the largest town in the region and a handy base for further exploration.

Day Two

Morning
The historical delights of Olsztyn's Stare Miasto and castle provide
adequate distraction to fill the morning. Lunch at one of the town's inviting
restaurants or cafés.

Afternoon and Evening
After lunch, head north towards the border with the Kaliningrad Enclave
to the mighty Gothic fortress at **6 Lidzbark Warmiński** (► 69–70). In
the evening retreat to Olsztyn to see the sights illuminated against the
dark night sky and end the day over a hearty meal at the Staromiejska
Restaurant (► 73).

Day Three

Morning
Pack your bags, say farewell to
Olsztyn and make a beeline south
to the small town of **7 Olsztynek**
(▶ 70) where you'll discover one of
Poland's best open-air museums
of folk architecture. Having
wandered the sandy tracks between
the timber buildings, have lunch at
the excellent Z Zielonym Piecem
Restaurant (▶ 73), then set off on
the long drive or train journey to
the village of Białowieża in the far
east of the country. With your own
set of wheels, you could drop in on
the picturesque town of **8 Pułtusk**
(right, ▶ 70) en route.

Evening
Having arrived at your base for the UNESCO-listed **3 Białowiesksi Park
Narodowy** (▶ 66–67), enjoy some hunter's fare at the Restauracja Carska
(▶ 72) and get a good night's sleep in preparation for next day's walk.

Day Four

Morning
Your first port of call should be the Forest Museum where you can learn
about the park (below) and its flora and fauna in a bit more detail. Then
take a guided trip into the park either on foot or by horse-drawn carriage,
or buy a map, rent a bicycle and set off to scout on your own.

Afternoon
If you failed to spot Białowieża's most celebrated resident in the forest
itself, pay the 300 or so bison at the Bison Reserve an afternoon visit. You
can finish the day back in Białowieża village with a stroll in Palace Park.

⬛ Kanal Ostródzko–Elbląski

The Ostródzko–Elbląski canal is a remarkable waterway for a number of reasons, most notably for the system of slipways it employs to get boats up and down inclines on dry land, but also for the bucolic countryside and bird-spotting territory it passes through on its way between the towns of Elbląg and Ostróda. Built to improve infrastructure in the region, it is now a popular tourist attraction.

Devised as a way of transporting timber from the Iława Lake area to the Baltic Sea, the 82km-long (50 miles) canal was built by Dutch engineer Georg Jakob Steenke in the mid-19th century and took 30 years to complete due to the many difficult obstacles the engineers had to surmount. The greatest of these is the 99.5m (326.3 feet) difference in water levels on a 10km (6-mile) stretch of the canal 20km (12 miles) from Elbląg. This problem was solved in a unique and ingenious way, not attempted anywhere else in Europe; boats are mounted on wheeled cradles, which lift them out of the water and haul them up and down the grassy inclines on rails. There are five such water-powered slipways on this stretch of the canal, constituting the high point of the trip and an extraordinary experience (passengers stay on board throughout). Tourists discovered the waterway in the 1930s and have been making the trip ever since, except for a break during World War II when the canal machinery was sabotaged. Timber shipments have long since ended and now the only vessels you'll see on the canal are pleasure boats and small private craft.

A boat navigating one of the steep slipways into the canal

Practical information

The 11-hour trip can be made in either direction with pleasure boats leaving both Elbląg and Ostróda early morning (May to September) and arriving in the evening. If you don't fancy spending all day on board, a good way to still see some picturesque countryside (Lake Drużno) and the slipways is to start in Elbląg and get off at Małdyty at the halfway point. For tickets, timetables and sailing information, contact the

Many tourists enjoy wildlife watching from the boat

Żegluga Ostródzko–Elbląska company in either town. A pair of binoculars for spotting birds on the banks, a packed lunch and warm clothes in spring and early autumn are good items to bring with you for the trip. Due to the early departures and late arrivals, it is usually necessary to stay in at least one of the towns at either end, and in the summer months the limited accommodation in these places should be booked well in advance.

TAKING A BREAK

On board you'll find a basic snack bar with teas, coffees, alcohol and snacks such as chocolate and sandwiches. It may be a good idea to pack a picnic lunch for something more substantial.

➕ 185 D3

Żegluga Ostródzko–Elbląska
Ostróda
➕ 185 E3 ✉ ul. Mickiewicza 9a ☎ 089 646 3871
Elbląg
➕ 185 D4 ✉ ul. Wieżowa ☎ 055 232 4307; www.zegluga.com.pl

KANAL OSTRÓDZKO–ELBLĄSKI: INSIDE INFO

Top tip Calling ahead for sailing information is particularly advisable in May, June and September as sailings can be cancelled if fewer than 20 passengers turn up. This rarely happens in the busiest months of July and August.

In more detail Lake Drużno is home to many species of bird and bird spotting is a good way to while away the lazy hours on board.

2 Olsztyn

With its engaging old town, attractive castle, relaxing riverside walks and nearby tourist attractions, the large town of Olsztyn is one of the best places to base yourself to explore the northeast. Only officially Polish since World War II, much of the town had to be rebuilt after liberation by the Red Army in 1945, though many important historical buildings survived.

Perhaps the best place to begin your tour of Olsztyn's attractions is at the neo-baroque **New Town Hall** at the busy crossroads to the north of the historical core, an impressive early 20th-century structure with a lofty clock tower and steep flowing gables. From there it's a short stroll along ul. 11. Listopada to the **High Gate**, the erstwhile entrance to the town through the long-since demolished town walls. Pass through its restored gateway to Olsztyn's main historical thoroughfare, **ul. Staromiejska**, a pleasant car-free stretch of cobbles lined with shops, cafes, restaurants and convenient benches. This brings you to the Rynek (market square) dominated by the **Old Town Hall** and lined with tall Prussian town houses sporting fancy gables. From the square, cut back across ul. Staromiejska and take any side street to reach the red-brick Gothic **Basilica of St James**, a monumental and atmospheric place of worship whose most striking features are the webbed Gothic ceiling and modern stained-glass windows.

Olsztyn's
Gothic castle

The cavernous interior of the Basilica of St James

To reach Olsztyn's *pièce de résistance,* the **Gothic castle** sitting high above the River Łyna, head back across the Rynek to ul. Zamkowa and cross the footbridge guarded by a bronze statue of Copernicus who once lived and worked here. The castle, part red-brick Teutonic fortress, part neoclassical rebuild, plays grand host to a branch of the Museum of Warmia and Mazury with exhibitions on Copernicus, local folk art, folk costumes and several smaller collections on regional themes.

TAKING A BREAK

Some of the top places to take a break are **Pierogarnia Bruner** on the Old Town Square (No. 26), ideal for a light lunch, and **Feniks Cafe** on busy ul. Prosta (No. 7) which serves a large selection of cakes, coffees and ice creams and has large show windows from which to watch Olsztyn bustle by.

➕ 185 F3

Tourist Information Office
✉ ul. Staromiejska 1 ☎ 089 535 3565; www.warmia-mazury-rot.pl

Castle Museum

Below left: Socialist realist artwork

✉ ul. Zamkowa 2 ☎ 089 527 9596; www.muzeum.olsztyn.pl ⏰ Summer daily 9–5; winter daily 10–4 💰 Inexpensive

---

OLSZTYN: INSIDE INFO

In more detail Olsztyn boasts an excellent **planetarium** (ul. Al. Marszałka J. Piłsudskiego 38, www.planetarium.olsztyn.pl) where heavenly shows take place daily in summer at noon and 2pm.

Hidden gem While exploring Olsztyn's old town centre, look up! What you'll see on many façades are weird and wonderful works of 1960s **socialist realist art**. Most examples of this style of painting and sculpture, popular with communist regimes, were removed in the 1990s but these frescoes, sgraffito and other decorative elements have survived.

❸ Białowieski Park Narodowy

Straddling the border with neighbouring Belarus, the Białowieski Forest was declared a national park in 1921, making it the oldest in Poland. Polish and foreign visitors alike come here to wander the 100sq km (39 square miles) of dense primeval woodland, declared a UNESCO World Heritage Site in 1979, in the hope of spotting animals that are rare in Europe including lynx, wolves, beavers and the greatest trophy of all, the European bison.

The Forest

Białowieski represents the last remnant of a forest that once covered the plains of Europe and provided a habitat for species that have long since disappeared from most European countries. After World War I it was discovered that only 50 bison had survived in zoos, which prompted the Polish government to declare the forest a protected area and reintroduce the bison into their last European home. The area was divided equally between Poland and Belarus after World War II; the Belarusian side today receives far fewer visitors than the Polish half.

Białowieski Village

The base for visiting the forest is the low-rise settlement of Białowieski, which sits in a large clearing. Here you'll find hotels and restaurants servicing the almost 100,000 visitors who travel here annually, as well as the park information

Typical wooden houses in the Białowieski area

point and agencies that can organise tours of the area. Other attractions in the village include the Palace Park laid out for Tsar Alexander III around a palace that was destroyed by the Nazis in 1944, the Eastern Orthodox Church of St Nicholas and the Forest Museum containing heaps of information on the surrounding area.

Visiting the Park

The park itself is divided into the Strictly Protected Area, which can only be visited with an official guide (prearranged with travel agencies in the village), and the rest of the forest which can be wandered at will. Guided tours are worth the expense as they visit the most interesting and atmospheric sections of the forest with the knowledgeable guides pointing out flora and fauna along the way. If you don't want to join an organised tour, a more easygoing way to tackle the park is to get hold of a local map showing all the hiking and cycling trails which crisscross the park, pack a picnic lunch and set off to explore at your own pace. For those who are pressed for time and want to see some of Białowieski's most famous residents close up, there's also a bison reserve situated around 4km (2.5 miles) to the west of the village.

Not all of the national park is forest – there are also tranquil meadows and streams

The best times to visit the park are autumn when the forest explodes in a blaze of colour, and winter when the snow lies deep on the ground and there are fewer people around. By far the worst time is early spring, when melting snow and rain turn the ground into a quagmire.

See the park from the comfort of a horse-drawn carriage

➕ 187 F2

Białowieski National Park Authority and Forest Museum
✉ Park Pałacowy 11 ☎ 085 682 9700; www.bpn.com.pl

BIAŁOWIESKI PARK NARODOWY: INSIDE INFO

Top tip A lazy way to see the forest is from one of the limited number of **horse-drawn carriages** permitted into the Strictly Protected Area every day. Booking ahead is advisable most of the year, essential in summer.

❹ Płock

The industrial town of Płock, perched high on a cliff top looking down on the mighty Vistula, is the oldest settlement in Mazovia, and from the 11th century was the de facto capital of Poland for 100 years. The appealing historical centre and some superb views make the town a worthy visit.

All Płock's attractions can be explored in half a day, beginning at the huge **cathedral**. Originally an 11th-century Romanesque structure, the building we see today is an 18th-century remodelling. The bronze doors are copies of the originals, which went missing for six centuries before mysteriously turning up in the Russian city of Novgorod.

Next door, make a short visit to the **Diocese Museum** before heading for the main branch of the **Regional Museum** at ul. Tumska 8, which has one of the best art nouveau exhibitions in the country. On leaving the museum, browse the shops on pedestrianised ul. Tumski before heading along ul. Grodzka to the Stary Rynek, where you can visit the tourist information centre. Płock's last attraction, the **Ethnographical Museum** (another branch of the Regional Museum) lies beyond the Rynek in a 19th-century granary.

The cathedral's octagonal spires loom over the historic centre

TAKING A BREAK

A couple of welcoming cafes occupy Płock's Stary Rynek. Try the arty music cafe **Czarny Kot** at No. 25 or **Vis-a-Vis** at No. 4, both of which have square-side seating in summer.

✚ 191 D4

Regional Museum
✉ ul. Tumska 8 ☎ 024 364 7071; www.muzeumplock.art.pl ⏰ Tue–Sun 10–5, closes earlier in winter 💰 Moderate

PŁOCK: INSIDE INFO

Hidden gem A **cliff-top path** runs from the Ethnographical Museum back to the cathedral area affording views of the Vistula, the opposite bank and the sandy beaches where most of the population decamps in the summer months.

At Your Leisure

5 Frombork

Tiny Frombork is best known as the place where Nicolaus Copernicus formulated his heliocentric theory of the solar system. He died here in 1543 and is buried in the cathedral though unfortunately nobody knows exactly where. The red-brick cathedral, with some baroque flourishes inside, stands on heavily fortified Cathedral Hill (Wzgórze Katedralne). It's the only real attraction in town and also home to the **Copernicus Museum** (Muzeum Kopernika) housed in the former Bishop's Palace. Here you can see exhibitions on Copernicus' life and work as well as other displays on telescopes, navigation and astronomy and interesting temporary exhibitions, normally with a scientific theme. The belfry in the southwest corner of the protective walls provides superb views as far as the Wiślana Lagoon on the Baltic coast (on clear days).

✚ 185 D4
Copernicus Museum
✉ ul. Katedralna 8 ☎ 055 244 0071;
www.frombork.art.pl ◷ Tue–Sun 9–4
🖐 Inexpensive

6 Lidzbark Warmiński

This small and fairly unremarkable town of 16,000 people 45km (28 miles) north of Olsztyn would warrant little attention were it not for the looming presence of one of the best-preserved Gothic red-brick castle in all Poland. Built in the late 14th century, the stocky square fortress, a tall turret at each corner, served as the main residence for the Warmian bishops until falling into disrepair in the 19th century. Renovated early in the last century, it emerged from World War II unscathed, unlike the town below which was almost wiped off the map.

The impressive bulk of Lidzbark Warmiński Castle

The self-guided tour starts in the cellars with their bare-brick walls and Gothic vaulting, after which you ascend to the first floor where various rooms contain portraits of the bishops and period furniture. The two most impressive spaces are the gold-themed rococo chapel, with its chessboard floor and cherubs fixed to Gothic vaulting, and the Great Refectory, a wonderful Gothic vaulted hall with fading frescoes, which houses an exhibition of local Gothic sculpture. More stairs bring visitors to two modernised levels used as an art gallery exhibiting an eclectic mix of Polish art from impressionism to almost the present day. The tour ends back on the courtyard surrounded on all sides by arcading and two levels of eye-catching loggia.

➕ 185 F4
Castle (Museum of Warmia in Lidzbark Warmiński)
✉ pl. Zamkowy 1 ☎ 089 767 2111; www.muzeum.olsztyn.pl ⏰ Tue–Sun 9–4
💰 Moderate

➐ Olsztynek Skansen

Around 30km (19 miles) south of Olsztyn on the northern edge of the small town of Olsztynek lies this delightful skansen or Open-Air Folk Architecture and Ethnographical Museum to give it its full title. Here, scattered among birch and pine trees

Wooden farmhouse, Olsztynek Skansen

Pułtusk's market square with the town hall at the far end

and connected by sandy pathways, you'll find farm buildings, a church, half-timbered houses, windmills and thatched cottages brought here primarily from Mazuria, Lithuania and Warmia and frozen in time to create snapshots of rural life in centuries gone by. During summer it's possible to enter most of the buildings containing period furniture and to watch the "locals" at work.

➕ 185 E3 ✉ ul. Sportowa 21 ☎ 089 519 2164; www.muzeumolsztynek.com.pl
⏰ Apr–Oct daily from 9; Apr, Sept & Oct closed Mon, grounds can be accessed free of charge in winter

➑ Pułtusk

Pułtusk, directly to the north of Warsaw, has had a long and turbulent history to say the least. Once home to the Płock bishops, it has suffered fires, the destructive 17th-century Swedish invasion, a major battle between the Russians and Napoleon and an even bigger clash involving the Red Army and the Nazis which left 80 per cent of its buildings in ruins. The town was even struck by a large meteorite in 1868! So it may come as a surprise to hear that Pułtusk is a relatively popular day-trip destination thanks to its attractive market square, the Stary Rynek (allegedly the longest in Europe), castle, Gothic church and regional museum housed in the Gothic tower of the town hall, mostly post-war rebuilds, of course.

➕ 186 A2

Where to... Stay

Prices

Expect to pay per night for a double room (in peak season):
€ under 200PLN €€ 200PLN–500PLN €€€ over 500PLN

BIAŁOWIESKI

Hotel Żubrówka Best Western €€

It doesn't get any better in the region than this four-star luxury place in the village of Białowieża, surrounded by the primeval forest. Snug bedrooms are packed with luxuries, most welcome after a long day bison-spotting in the forest. The hotel also has spa facilities, a plush restaurant, smiling service and many other little touches to make your visit to the national park as pleasant as possible.

🚇 187 F2 ☒ ul. Olgi Gabiec 6 ☎ 085 681 2303; www.hotel-zubrowka.pl

ELBLĄG

Hotel Młyn €€

The most popular pre-canal trip option in Elbląg must be the Młyn, imaginatively constructed from the burned-out shell of a large former watermill (młyn is Polish for mill). The 26 cheery and modern rooms are designed to satisfy travellers' every need, with squeaky-clean bathrooms, large beds, satellite TV, fridge and internet access. The on-site restaurant is the ideal breakfast stop before being wafted aboard.

🚇 185 D4 ☒ ul. Kościuszki 132 ☎ 055 235 0470; www.hotelmlyn.com.pl

OLSZTYN

Pod Zamkiem €€

This characterful 17-room family-run hotel occupies a listed art nouveau villa set in parkland below the castle. Rooms of various shapes and sizes come with en suite facilities and TV and some enjoy views of the castle. Most are clustered around a spooky-castle-style landing which looks down onto a cosy reception area with bar and original ceramic stove. Personality and intimacy make this the best place to sleep in town.

🚇 185 F3 ☒ ul. Nowowiejskiego 10 ☎ 089 535 1287; www.hotel-olsztyn.com.pl

OSTRÓDA

Promenada €

Canal explorers in need of a bed for the night at the other end could do worse than the modern but rather uninspiring Promenada near the quay and stations. Rooms are of a decent standard but no luxury, and as Ostróda is an altogether unexceptional town, you'll probably not be hanging around here long anyway.

🚇 185 E3 ☒ ul. Mickiewicza 3 ☎ 089 642 8100 www.hotelpromenada.pl

PŁOCK

Starzyński €€

The building of the Starzyński may display some obvious features of communist-era architectural style, but its the best place to stay in town and enjoys a prime location overlooking the Vistula, the cathedral and the town's new riverside amphitheatre. Rooms are well appointed and some have awe-inspiring views of the main attractions. The hotel also prides itself on its plush restaurant serving a mix of Polish and international favourites. Noise could be an issue if there's an event at the amphitheatre below.

🚇 191 D4 ☒ ul. Piekarska 1 ☎ 024 366 0200; www.starzynski.com.pl

Where to...
Eat and Drink

Prices

Expect to pay for a three-course meal for one, excluding drinks:
€ under 50PLN   €€ 50PLN–100PLN   €€€ over 100PLN

BIAŁOWIESKI

Restauracja Carska €€

Dine like Dr Zhivago or Anna Karenina at this new, intriguing and highly recommended throwback to imperial Russia occupying the dinky log building of the old railway station. There are four dining rooms to choose from with the Tsar's Room, the Hunter's Salon, the Romantic Salon and the Representative Main Hall, each decorated according to the theme with portraits of Tsar Nicholas II, hunting trophies and Russian oil paintings. Do not be put off by the restaurant's rather formal atmosphere – this place is usually full of fleece-clad walkers in muddy boots. Needless to say, the menu is a mixture of Polish and Russian staple dishes.

➕ 187 F2 ☒ ul. Stacja Towarowa 4 ☎ 085 681 2119 ⏰ Daily 10–1c

ELBLĄG

Słowiańska €€

Elbląg's finest dining establishment is a welcome sight at the end of an 11-hour canal trip, or a great place to start the day before a cruise. The interior is a mix of Polish chintz and clean-cut contemporary décor and the menu is also an unusual blend of local Polish and Italian (*kuchnia włoska* in Polish). Diners can choose from pasta dishes, *frutti di mare* or locally hunted game for their main meal, though you may want to give the bison (*żubr*, not caught locally) in hunter's sauce a miss. The hot apple cake with ice cream is a real Polish treat with which to end your meal and the Słowiańska has one of the best-stocked bars in town.

➕ 185 D4 ☒ ul. Krótka 4 ☎ 055 611 4702 ⏰ Daily noon–last customer

Pod Aniołami €€

If you've had your fill of pierogi and vodka, "Under the Angels" comes as a pleasant and spicy surprise with its Latin American menu and large selection of tequilas. There are two halls to choose from where guests are (hopefully) transported to South America and there's outdoor seating in summer. The food is well prepared though purists will be able to taste the Polish touch.

➕ 185 D4 ☒ ul. Rybacka 23/24B ☎ 055 236 1726 ⏰ Daily 11–midnight

OSTRÓDA

Tawerna Mariaszek €

Housed in a timber structure rising on stilts above the Młyński Canal, the chunky wood interior is as good a place as any in Ostróda to enjoy some belly-warming Polish fare and a cool *piwo* after a long day on a boat. The menu features a good selection of fish and traditional meat dishes but there's little for vegetarians. The terrace overlooking the water is a pleasant spot to unwind on summer evenings.

➕ 185 E3 ☒ ul. Drewniana ☎ 089 640 5293 ⏰ Daily 10am–last customer

OLSZTYN

Przystań €€

The timber-built Przystań on the banks of Ukiel Lake, around 1.5km

(1 mile) from the historical centre, must take the title of northeast Poland's biggest eatery, as it is capable of hosting 500 diners indoors and 2,000 on the decking outside. The international menu is fish- and meat-heavy, though some allowances are made for non-carnivores in the shape of fried cheese and savoury pancakes. A bit of a hike from the centre but worth it on warm summer evenings.

🚩 185 F3 🚇 ul. Żeglarska ☎ 089 523 7779 🕙 Daily 11–11

Rożana €€

Oak-panelled walls, flower and lace décor, courteous well-presented waiters and a homey ambience are what discerning diners have been enjoying at the Rose Café, tucked away in a corner of the former fish market, since it opened in 2003. The menu includes imaginative takes on Polish staples such as boar in rose and cranberry sauce and rabbit with mashed beetroot. Wash down delicious dishes with a vintage red or white from the extensive wine list although here a rosé may be more in order.

🚩 185 F3 🚇 Targ Rybny 14 ☎ 089 523 5039 🕙 Daily 10am–last customer

Staromiejska €€

Olsztyn's best-known and most central restaurant is a neat and tidy affair with a 19th-century ambience and hints of its communist-era days here and there. Whether you seat yourself indoors, under the arcading or on the Rynek itself, refuel on rich Polish dishes such as duck, hunter's goulash, pierogi and fish, or a selection of meat-free meals, among the hubbub of other diners. This is also an ideal spot for a hot coffee and delicious gâteau.

🚩 185 F3 🚇 Stare Miasto 4/6 ☎ 089 527 5883 🕙 Daily 10–10

OLSZTYNEK

Z Zielonym Piecem €

Taking its name from the huge green stove (zielony piec) that dominates the four-table dining room, this undiscovered gem of a restaurant is well worth seeking out. Typical chintzy Polish floweriness is the dominating theme but the food, made entirely from locally sourced organic ingredients, is out of this world and a real treat for the tastebuds. The handwritten menus have a seasonal flavour so in autumn expect mushroom sauces and thick wild berry jam, while in winter, meat, fish and warming soups are the order of the day. The owners are committed to giving guests an authentic rural dining experience and they have plans to open a shop-cum-café on the main square with a similar philosophy.

🚩 185 E3 🚇 ul. Floriana 1 ☎ 089 519 1081 🕙 Daily noon–9pm

Karczma w Skansenie €€

A convenient but obviously touristy place to eat is this tavern housed in a large 18th-century hall next to the skansen ticket office. Generous portions of meat and fish are served among rural farmyard clutter in a hall-timber setting by waitresses in countryside garb (though you may well have to compete with a German tour bus party for their attention). Unfortunately, this place shuts up shop over winter.

🚩 185 E3 🚇 ul. Lesna 20 ☎ 089 519 3555 🕙 Daily 10–8

PŁOCK

Art Deco €€

The obvious choice on Płock's main square is this simple, clean-cut eatery where you can enjoy generous portions of Polish pork, imaginatively prepared fish dishes, duck or just pierogi either indoors or, when the sun shines, out on the square itself. Staff do not speak much English and the menu is in Polish only, but foreign diners normally get by.

🚩 191 D4 🚇 Stary Rynek 17 ☎ 024 268 5751 🕙 Daily 10am–last customer

Where to...
Shop

The northeast is not exactly a shopper's delight though you may find some interesting souvenirs at the region's tourist hotspots.

SOUVENIRS

Among the best places to pick up souvenirs and crafts are the stalls by the entrance to the Olsztynek Skansen, or just outside the Bison Reserve near Białowieski, where sellers offer local handicrafts such as embroidered linen, hand-woven baskets and items made from straw and grass. There are also branches of Cepelia, the nationwide network of handicrafts shops, in Olsztyn (ul. Prosta 1), Płock (ul. Miodowa 4) and Elbląg (ul. 1 Maja 14).

Where to...
Be Entertained

There's always something going on in the northeast, especially in summer, when music festivals and concerts fill squares and churches. Off season, you can retreat to the cinema or ask at the tourist information office about any local events taking place.

MUSIC

One of the most respected classical music bodies in the northeast is the Feliks Nowowiejski Philharmonia orchestra based in Olsztyn (www.filharmonia.olsztyn.pl). Romantic composer Chopin came from Mazovia, and the region is known for its traditional music, such as the mazurka and polonaise. Płock, the

major town in western Mazovia, has a regular programme of classical music concerts performed by the Płock Symphony Orchestra (www.posorkiestra.pl) at the PSM Concert Hall (ul. Kolegialna 23). The town also holds a two-month-long Summer Music Festival in July and August which takes place at a number of venues around the town, including the cathedral, the amphitheatre and the Stary Rynek. The Płock Choir Festival is one of the best in Europe and is held annually in late March.

OLSZTYN SUMMER FESTIVALS

Every summer from mid-June through to September, Olsztyn

hosts a summer cultural festival at various venues around the town. Events range from organ concerts at the cathedral and poetry readings to motorcycle displays. The festival overlaps with the Olsztyn Blues Nights festival in July (www.olsztynskielatoartystyczne.pl, www.blues.olsztyn.pl)

CINEMA

The best cinemas in the region can be found in Olsztyn (Helios, al. Piłsudskiego 16), Białystok (Helios, ul. Czesława Miłosza 2) and Pułtusk (Kino Narew, pl. Teatralny 4). Films are often shown in their original language with Polish subtitles, but it's best to check first.

WHAT'S ON

Local tourist information centres are generally the best places to contact to find out what events are taking place when you are planning to be in town.

Kraków

Getting Your Bearings

Poland's glorious former capital and best preserved historical city deserves to be the country's main tourist attraction and is an essential element in any tour of central Europe. With its full house of architectural styles ranging from Romanesque to art nouveau, its crooked atmospheric streets, hilltop castle complex and profusion of bars and restaurants, UNESCO-listed Kraków, which was hardly affected by World War II, is often compared to the Czech capital, Prague. A couple of days strolling the handsome city centre, exploring the Wawel Hill and nosing around museums and galleries will give you an insight into Poland's rich cultural heritage and proud history.

Unlike Poland's present-day capital, Kraków is easily navigable for the first-timer with the city centre retaining its medieval layout. The heart of the city is Rynek Główny, a huge market square from which streets peel off in all directions. Ul. Floriańska, one of Poland's most exclusive and historically interesting thoroughfares, heads north while ul. Grodzka leads south to Wawel Hill, atop which sit the former royal castle and cathedral. Encircling the centre is the Planty, a ring of 19th-century parkland

Page 75: Town hall tower lit up at night

★ Don't Miss

1 Rynek Główny and
   Around ➤ 80
2 Wawel ➤ 84
3 Kazimierz ➤ 88

At Your Leisure

4 Nowa Huta ➤ 90
5 Zwierzyniec ➤ 90
6 Las Wolski ➤ 91
7 Tyniec ➤ 91

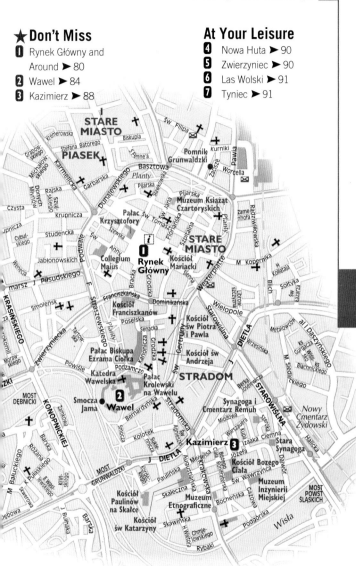

**Page 75:
The town
hall tower
in Kraków's
market square**

where hefty defensive walls once protected the city from
attack. The Planty is lined with a ring road, which keeps
traffic out of the partly pedestrianised old centre. To the
southeast lies the former Jewish quarter and erstwhile separate
town of Kazimierz, an up-and-coming district of old Jewish
monuments interspersed with interesting bars and restaurants.
Kraków also possesses some undervisited suburbs, most
notably Nowa Huta, a post-war Stalinist creation purpose-
built around a huge steelworks.

In Three Days

If you're not quite sure where to begin your travels, this itinerary recommends a practical and enjoyable three days in Kraków, taking in some of the best places to see using the Getting Your Bearings map on the previous page. For more information see the main entries.

Day One

Morning
Visitors on their first day in Kraków cannot fail to be drawn by the tourist magnet which is the ❶ **Rynek Główny** (left; ➤ 80–83), so start the day over coffee and pastries at one of its many atmospheric cafes. After breakfast, head directly for the nearest tourist information office to pick up your Kraków Card (➤ 82), an essential companion for the next three days. You'll have your first chance to use it at the Church of St Mary, then it's across to the Sukiennice (left) to pick up some souvenirs before a stroll along ul. Floriańska to see the Barbakan and Florian Gate. You'll be spoiled for choice when it comes to lunchtime, but a light affair outdoors on the Rynek is normally a winner.

Afternoon and Evening
After lunch climb to the top of ❷ **Wawel Hill** (➤ 84–87), to spend the rest of the day discovering this fascinating complex, once the seat of royal and spiritual power in Poland. End the day at one of Kraków's superb city-centre restaurants.

Day Two

Morning
Kick off the day in ❸ **Kazimierz** (➤ 88–89), where a tour of the former Jewish religious sites, a couple of Christian churches (opposite, top) and museums will work up an appetite which can be satisfied at the Jewish Dawno Temu na Kazimierzu restaurant (➤ 93).

Afternoon and Evening

After lunch, museums are on the menu for the afternoon with the unmissable Czartoryski Museum (➤ 82) your first stop. After dinner, end the day with a classical music performance or something more casual such as an evening at a jazz club.

Day Three

Morning

Escape the tourist throngs of the historical core in an East German Trabant, the quirky vehicle used by Communism Tours to transport visitors around the Stalinist-era delights of **4** Nowa Huta (➤ 90).

Afternoon and Evening

After a proletariat-style lunch in a basic communist-era milk-bar (part of the tour), head west to the suburb of **5** Zwierzyniec (➤ 90) to clamber up the Kościuszko Mound (below) for a bird's eye view of the entire city.

❶ Rynek Główny and Around

Kraków's main market square, measuring 200m by 200m (218 by 218 yards), was the largest in Europe when it was laid out in 1257. Lined with grandiose town houses whose neoclassical facades hide Gothic and Renaissance interiors, the square buzzes day and night with tourists, street cafés and people out on the tiles, and is the true heart of Poland's most attractive city. The two main attractions are the Church of St Mary, which stands at an angle to the rest of the square, and the Sukiennice (Cloth Hall), which dominates the centre. Head along any street leading off the square to discover atmospheric alleyways, tucked away churches and cobbled streets, which have changed little in 200 years.

Kościół Mariacki (Church of St Mary)

Constructed in red brick at the end of the 14th century to replace the original church razed to the ground by the Tatars in 1241, Kraków's most striking church is most notable from the outside for possessing two very dissimilar spires. The legend behind this goes that these towers were the work of two brothers who competed to see who could build highest. The brother who lost murdered his sibling in a fit of jealousy but then, wracked with remorse, committed suicide by throwing himself off his tower. If you are around the church on the hour, you will hear a bugler playing the *hejnał* (bugle call) from the top of one of the spires, a tradition going back to the Tatar

invasion. Seeing the enemy at the gates, the watchman tried to warn the townsfolk of the impending danger but was cut short by a Tatar arrow, hence the rather abrupt end to the piece which is played four times, once to each side of the city.

Despite the plain brick exterior, inside the church you are met by a riot of decoration and colour with stained glass windows and star-speckled ceiling. The highlight, however, is one of Kraków's most celebrated works of art, the **late Gothic altarpiece** created by Nuremburg sculptor **Veit Stoss** (Wit Stwosz in Polish) between 1477 and 1489. Some of Poland's most celebrated artists also

The Veit Stoss altar in St Mary's Church

contributed to the interior: see the friezes by Matejko and art nouveau stained glass by Wyspiański.

Sukiennice

This grand medieval market building, whose name translates as Cloth Hall, appeared in the very middle of the Rynek as early as the 14th century and has remained virtually unchanged since it gained some Renaissance touches in the mid 16th century. The huge complex contains a couple of attractions, but the chief draw for most is the internal covered street which runs the length of the building and is lined with **souvenir stalls** selling possibly the widest range of authentic gifts (and mass produced tack) in the country. **The Gallery of 19th-century Polish Art** on the eastern flank provides some highbrow culture for those less interested in taking home a reproduction medieval broadsword or portrait of the late Pope John Paul II in imitation amber. The area around the Sukiennice is also the focus for seasonal events

Left: Rynek Głowny at night, with the Sukiennice and town hall tower illuminated

such as Christmas and Easter markets. The Sukiennice once shared centre stage with the old town hall, the only reminder of which is the adjacent 70m-tall (230-foot) **Town Hall Tower**, the best vantage point from which to survey Kraków's historical core.

Browsing through the stalls in the Sukiennice

North of Rynek Główny

The grand medieval thoroughfare extending north from the Rynek is **ul. Floriańska**, once part of the Royal Way. Polish kings would enter the city from the north through the **Barbakan** and the **Florian Gate** and make their way along ul. Floriańska to the Rynek and on to Wawel Castle. Today this is the city centre's busiest pedestrian street, lined with bars, restaurants, hotels and fashionable boutiques. The **Czartoryski Museum**, one of Poland's best art museums, is located a block west. If you are going to visit just one museum in Kraków, this should be it as the collections of ancient art from Egypt and Greece and the exhibition of Polish, Flemish and Italian masters are first-rate. The museum's pride and joy is Leonardo da Vinci's *Lady with an Ermine*.

RYNEK GŁÓWNY: INSIDE INFO

Top tip A **Kraków Card** is a must-have for anyone planning two or three days of active sightseeing in the city. The card entitles the holder to free travel on public transport, entry to 30 museums including the Czartoryski Museum, St Mary's Church and all branches of the Kraków National Museum (but not the Wawel complex) and some less attractive discounts at selected restaurants. Cards, valid for two or three days, can be purchased at any tourist information centre, eight of the best-known travel agencies and from many hotels. For more information, log on to www.krakowcard.com.

South of Rynek Główny

Ul. Grodzka takes over from ul. Floriańska on the southern flank of the Rynek and runs from the square to the base of Wawel Hill. The Baroque **Church of SS Peter and Paul** (Kościół św. Piotra i Pawła) and the ancient twin-towered Romanesque **Church of St Andrew** (Kościół św. Andrzeja) and many other religious buildings provide architectural distraction as you approach the Wawel.

TAKING A BREAK

Countless cafés clutter Rynek Główny with their posh garden furniture and logo-bearing sunshades. Sit out on the square in the summer months but in winter retreat to warm and welcoming interiors. The best are **Cafe Europejski** at No. 35, **Redolfi** at No. 38, **Kawarnia Bankowa** at No. 47 and **Bar Szara at No. 6** near the Church of St Mary.

✚ 200 B4

Kościól Mariackl (Church of St Mary)
✚ 200 B4 🕓 Mon–Sat 11:30–6, Sun 2–6 ✋ Moderate

The Barbakan seen through the Florian Gate

Muzeum Książąt Czartoryskich (Czartoryski Museum)
✚ 200 B5 ✉ ul. Św. Jana 19 ☎ 012 422 5566 🕓 Summer Tue–Sat 10–6, Sun 10–4; shorter hours in winter ✋ Moderate, free Sun

2 Wawel

Wawel Hill, rising above the River Vistula in the southern part of Kraków's historical centre, is Poland's most historically significant attraction and if you were pressed to choose just one place to visit in the entire country, this would have to be it. The magnificent complex, made up of the Royal Castle, the Wawel Cathedral and various museums, was for six centuries the seat of Polish kings who ruled the land from this suitably elevated location.

Pałac Królewski (Royal Castle)

There is evidence to suggest that Wawel Hill was home to a royal residence as early as the 10th century, but the castle we see today dates from the early 16th century when King Sigismund Stary employed Italian architect Bertomeo Berrecci to convert his draughty Gothic abode into a majestic Renaissance palazzo. Following King Sigismund III Vasa's decision to move the capital to Warsaw, the castle fell into a state of disrepair and over the centuries was used by the Austrians as a barracks and the Nazis as an official residence. The last attack on the fabric of the building came in the post-war years in the form of acid rain caused to a large extent by the construction of the nearby Nowa Huta steelworks. Despite use and abuse, the Royal Castle has survived to tell the tale and has undergone renovation work to return it to its former splendour.

The castle is divided into the **State Rooms** (Komnaty Królewskie), the **Treasury** (Skarbiec), the **Oriental Art Exhibition** (Wystawa Sztuka Wschodu) and the **Lost Wawel Exhibition** (Wystawa Wawel Zaginiony), with a separate ticket needed for each. In addition there is a special tour available of the **Private Royal Apartments** (Prywatne

The view across the Vistula to Wawel Castle

The castle's inner courtyard with its triple row of arcades

Apartamenty Królewskie) which is limited to 10 people at a time and needs to be booked well in advance. The tour shows visitors the opulent rooms inhabited by the monarch as well as chambers used by his guests, all chock-a-block with period furniture and artwork. Most, however, take the standard guided tour of the State Rooms, which begins on the arcaded courtyard and visits a series of grand Gothic, Renaissance and baroque halls, rooms and chambers littered with period furniture and huge Flanders tapestries. After the tour, your next stop should be the Treasury where some of the surviving crown jewels, the coronation sword and period military exhibits are displayed in a series of Gothic rooms. If you've still got the energy, the Oriental Art Exhibition in the west wing is a display of items relating to Poland's trade and military contacts with the Near East (Persian carpets, Turkish military banners, Chinese vases) while the Lost Wawel Exhibition deals with archaeological digs and finds on Wawel Hill. You may want to miss these last two minor attractions in favour of saving your legs for the cathedral.

Katedra Wawelska (Wawel Cathedral)

Immediately to the west of the castle rises Wawel Cathedral. A church first appeared here in 1020, but every ruler and era since that time has added to the original Romanesque church (parts of which still survive) so sturdy Gothic red brick vies for the onlooker's attention with baroque swirls and Renaissance elaboration. In addition to serving for almost a thousand years as the epicentre of religious life in Poland, the cathedral was also where Polish kings were crowned and where 41 of their number and several more recent statesmen are buried.

Wawel Cathedral is an eclectic mix of architectural styles

Just as you enter the cathedral, notice the set of prehistoric animal bones at the entrance, which, legend would have us believe, belonged to the Krak dragon. The bones guarantee the safety of the cathedral and must never be removed. Enter the cathedral to be greeted by a riot of decoration, vaulting, chapels, tombs and altars. The **nave** is packed with the tombs of various kings, bishops and the nobility and lined with ornate side chapels, the most impressive of which is the 16th-century Sigismund Chapel (Kaplica Zygmuntowska) in green sandstone and red marble. Having explored the nave, ascend the 14th-century **Sigismund Tower** (Wieża Zygmuntowska) for a look at the Sigismund bell, the biggest in Poland weighing in at 11 tonnes (12.1 tons), and to admire

the panoramic view of the city from the top. Next, descend to the **crypt** where inscriptions on the many tombstones read like a who's who of Polish history. As well as notable and lesser known kings and queens, the greatest Polish poet Adam Mickiewicz, 18th-century military leader Tadeusz Kościuszko and interwar president and dictator Józef Piłsudski are also buried here. The only other attraction is the **cathedral museum** (Muzeum Katedralne), which is only of limited interest.

Wawel's fearsome dragon, Smok, still breathes out fire today for the benefit of the tourists

Other Attractions

According to legend, the curious **Dragon's Den** (Smocza Jama) situated in the western slope of Wawel Hill was once the cave home of a fire-breathing monster that terrorised the townsfolk of Kraków and demanded they bring a certain number of cattle for it to eat every week. One day, a clever cobbler called Skuba decided to get rid of the creature once and for all. He filled a sheep's carcass with lime and left it outside the cave. The dragon swallowed it whole and, feeling a fire in his belly, dived into the Vistula to quench his thirst and exploded. The cave can be accessed by special lift from the southwestern ramparts and having explored the three chambers you emerge onto the banks of the Vistula to be greeted by a sculpture of the dragon.

The recently opened **Royal Gardens** found atop the eastern wall are a faithful reconstruction of a small Renaissance garden complex.

The Sigismund bell – touch its clapper and you will be lucky in love

TAKING A BREAK

The **Kaviarnia pod Basztą** next to the tourist and ticket centre is the only place for a cappuccino or sandwich, though most visitors usually head back down the hill for more choice.

🔢 200 A3

Wawel Ticket Office
☎ 012 422 5155; www.wawel.krakow.pl
🕐 Daily 9–4

Palac Krolewski na Wawelu (Royal Castle)
🕐 Summer Mon 9:30–1, Tue–Fri 9:30–5, Sat–Sun 11–6; shorter hours and closed Mon in winter 💷 Expensive, free entry Mon in Summer

Katedra Wawelska (Cathedral)
🕐 Mon–Sat 9–5, Sun 12:30–5 💷 Free except Royal tombs, Sigismund bell and Museum (moderate)

Dragon's Den
🕐 Apr–Oct daily 10–5 💷 Inexpensive; free for under 7s

WAWEL: INSIDE INFO

Top tip In high season the attractions on Wawel Hill can be hopelessly overcrowded and as visitor numbers are restricted, just turning up on the day may mean you won't see a thing. To avoid disappointment, **call ahead** at least the day before to book tickets, which you should collect 20 minutes before your allotted tour is due to depart.

One to miss Unless you have a particular interest in Polish ecclesiastical history you shouldn't feel guilty about missing the **Cathedral Museum** opposite the cathedral's main entrance.

❸ Kazimierz

Roughly defined by the Vistula, the Jewish cemetery and wide ul. Dietla, the former Jewish quarter of Kazimierz is an up-and-coming district of antique Jewish heritage sites, quirky boutiques and arty cafés.

The cobbled streets and alleyways of this once separate town have a slightly dilapidated, timeless feel and possess enough character to transport visitors back, momentarily at least, to pre-war days, despite the once 60,000 strong Jewish community having been whittled down to just a few hundred members by Nazi death camps and decades of communism. Steven Spielberg found the location so authentic he shot many scenes from the film *Schindler's List* at various locations around Kazimierz.

Jewish Sights

Kazimierz's Jewish sites are grouped together in a rectangle between ul. Krakowska and ul. Starowiślna and can be explored in half a day. Possibly the best place to start is the **Old Synagogue** (Stara Synagoga), at the southern end of ul. Szeroka, which has been converted into the **Jewish Museum**. On the right-hand side of the wide street you will find the **Remuh Synagogue** and **Cemetery** which can both be visited when services are not taking place. At the end of ul. Szeroka, notice the **Klezmer Hois Hotel**, once the site of the *mikvah* (ritual bathhouse) and now home to a kosher restaurant. The olde-worlde faux shop fronts of one of Kazimierz's best eateries, Dawno temu na Kazimierzu, can be found opposite.

At the top of ul. Szeroka, take a left into ul. Miodowa to visit the 19th-century, neo-Romanesque **Tempel Synagogue** with its stained glass and ornate interior. From there head south along ul. Estery via Plac Novy to ul. Isaaka where the 17th-century **Isaac Synagogue** (Synagoga Izaaka), Kraków's largest, is home to yet another museum with an exhibition on the history of Polish Jews. It's a short hop from there to the **High Synagogue** (Synagoga Wysoka), so called due to its first-floor prayer room.

Christian Sights

Western Kazimierz was never inhabited by the Jewish community and therefore boasts a handful of impressive churches. The **Skałka Church** (Kościół Paulinów

Tempel Synagogue is more colourful and ornate inside than the area's older synagogues

The Gothic facade of Corpus Christi Church

na Skałce) in parkland near the Vistula is associated with the martyrdom of St Stanisław, bishop of Kraków, in 1079 and also contains the grave of painter Stanisław Wyspiański. The 14th-century **Church of St Catherine** (Kościół św. Katarzyny) in ul. Skałeczna is a colossal red-brick affair though the interior is rather bare. The **Corpus Christi Church** (Kościół Bożego Ciała) on ul. Bożego Ciała dates from the late 14th century and still boasts stained glass fitted at the time as well as many baroque additions.

TAKING A BREAK

Ul. Szeroka is lined with cafés and restaurants, many with a Jewish theme. **Plac Nowy** also has its fair share of street-side tables, which look onto the old Jewish slaughterhouse in the middle, though inside these tend to be earthier affairs.

✛ 200 C2

Jewish Museum
✉ Stara Synagoga, ul. Szeroka 24 ☎ 012 422 0962 🕐 Mon 10–2, Wed, Thu, Sat, Sun 9–4, Fri 10–5 💰 Moderate, free on Mondays

KAZIMIERZ: INSIDE INFO

In more depth The Galicja Jewish Museum at ul. Dajwór 18 (012 421 6842; www.galiciajewishmuseum.org) is an exhibition by award-winning photographer Chris Schwarz of 135 images depicting Jewish life in southern Poland post-Holocaust. Photographs of abandoned synagogues, forgotten cemeteries and the infamous death camps are a powerful reminder of the horrific events that took place here just six decades ago.

At Your Leisure

4 Nowa Huta

The Kraków suburb of Nowa Huta, 10km (6 miles) east of the city centre, was built almost from scratch in the 1940s and 1950s to accommodate workers from then new Nowa Huta steelworks. The entire project was designed to break Kraków's intellectual and spiritual backbone by plonking a huge slab of proletariat on its doorstep. Today, a stroll along its wide Soviet-style boulevards lined with **Stalinist neo-renaissance architecture** shows an alternative side to the city few tourists see.

To get to Nowa Huta, take tram 4 or tram 15 for the 30-minute or so journey from the main railway station to Plac Centralny. This is the main square (its full and rather comical name being Plac Centralny im. Ronalda Reagana) from which avenues hemmed by seven-floor Stalinist tenements shoot off in all directions. The suburb's only real tourist site is the fascinating **Arka Pana Church** in ul. Obrońców Krzyża, built in the 1970s after, somewhat ironically, much lobbying by the population who were meant to break the city's Catholic traditions. The pebble-encrusted church, which vaguely resembles an ark, was financed entirely from contributions and built by volunteers with no assistance from the state, unimaginable in most other communist countries at the time.

A special marked trail called the *trasa nowohucka* starts at the steelworks (no access to the public) and makes its winding way to the Arka Pana Church via nine other places of interest. Communism Tours (www.crazyguides.com) also run fun Trabant tours to Nowa Huta for small groups of visitors.

➕ 196 A3
Tourist Information Office
✉ os. Słoneczne 16 ☎ 012 643 0303

The Cross on the roof of Arka Pana Church, Nowa Huta

5 Zwierzyniec

Extending west from the city centre, the only reason to head out to the suburb of Zwierzyniec, one of Kraków's oldest quarters, is to climb the **Kościuszko Mound**. This 100m-high (328 feet) cone of earth was created in the early 1820s in honour of Tadeusz Kościuszko, Polish resistance leader and hero of the American War of Independence. The mound stands atop the highest hill in the area and from the top the panoramic views of the city in its entirety are spectacular and well worth the legwork to get up there. Look out for the Wawel by the river and the Nowa Huta steelworks beyond, and notice how the tiny historical centre is lost in a sea of drab prefab estates which most foreigners never see.

To get to the mound, take tram 1, 2 or 6 to the terminus at Salwator then walk the 1.6km (1 mile) up the hill or hop on hourly bus 100, which stops at the foot of the mound. There is a charge to climb the mound itself,

The top of the Kościuszko Mound

though the views are free from a nearby terrace.

🚩 200 A3 (off map)
Kościuszko Mound
🕐 May–Sep 9am–dusk 💰 Expensive

🔟 Las Wolski

Las Wolski (or Wolski Forest) is an expanse of relaxing woodland on the western outskirts of the city, popular among Cracovians as a place to picnic, relax, jog, cycle and pick mushrooms. If you're spending more than a few days in Kraków, the greenery and birdsong can be a relaxing antidote to the multitudes of tourists in the historical centre. Other than unwinding and picnicking, there's not a lot else to do here apart from visiting the local zoo or climbing yet another mound, this time dedicated to interwar Polish leader, Józef Piłsudski. Take bus 134 to the zoo.

🚩 196 A3

🔟 Tyniec

The small village of Tyniec on the southwestern edge of Kraków is popular with Polish summer day-trippers thanks to the Benedictine abbey perched high on a limestone cliff by the Vistula. The abbey is something of a survivor having been burnt down by the Tatars in the 12th century, the Swedes 400 years later and the Russians in the 18th century. Today the church and its summer organ recitals are of greatest interest.

🚩 196 A3 📧 112

Tyniec Abbey was founded in the 11th century but has been rebuilt many times

Where to... Stay

Prices

Expect to pay per night for a double room (in peak season):

€ under 200PLN   €€ 200PLN–500PLN   €€€ over 500PLN

Andels €€€

What's good enough for Prague is good enough for Kraków, and this spanking new 159-room design hotel, whose sister establishment opened in the Czech capital in 2002, is set to become one of the trendiest places to stay in Poland. Housed in a limb of the glass-and-steel Galeria Krakowska near Kraków's main railway station, the Kraków Andels shares much with its Prague sibling such as cutting-edge room design and top-class facilities, DVD, flat screen TV and CD player in every room.

➕ 200 C5 ✉ ul. Pawia 3 ☎ 012 660 0100;
www.andelscracow.com

Hotel Stary €€€

This former aristocratic residence is one of Poland's finest hotels, and if you are looking to splash out and treat someone, then this is the place to do it. Rooms are incredibly spacious and some even have modest views of Rynek Główny as well as a Jacuzzi in the Italian marble bathroom and a truly opulent feel. Under the hotel you'll discover a magnificent vaulted cellar pool, part of a fitness club which boasts its own salt cave. This hotel may have hefty room rates but it is worth it.

➕ 200 A4 ✉ ul. Szczepańska 5
☎ 012 384 0808; www.stary.hotel.com.pl

Maltański €€€

This small, understated 16-room hotel is a classic affair with almost boutique rooms and personal service hard to find in Poland. Parquet floors, dark wood furniture, light textiles and a tranquil atmosphere make staying at the Maltański a relaxing experience. The hotel is just a five-minute stroll through the Planty to the Rynek Główny yet enjoys a quite location away from the crowds. The company own four other hotels including the exquisite 14th-century Korzkiew Castle, a truly magnificent getaway 13 km (9 miles) from Kraków, with beautiful interiors and stunning forest views.

➕ 200 A3 ✉ ul. Straszewskiego 14
☎ 012 431 0010; www.donimirski.com

Pod Różą €€€

Occupying a prime spot on Kraków's most famous street, you won't find a more central place to stay in the city, nor one with more history behind it. The oldest hotel in Kraków has hosted royalty and celebrity over the centuries including Tsar Alexander I and Franz Liszt. Today its 57 antique dotted rooms are full of character as well as boasting state-of-the-art facilities. Possibly the finest place to stay in all of Kraków.

➕ 200 B4 ✉ ul. Floriańska 14 ☎ 012 424 3300; www.hotel.com.pl

Pugetów €€€

Located around 400m (436 yards) southeast of the Rynek Główny and taking its name from the nearby Pugetów Palace, this boutique hotel is run by the same company as the Maltański and has much of the same charm and elegance. Each classy room behind the neoclassical facade has been individually designed and named after a personality from Poland's history. There's also a cellar restaurant over which arches atmospheric red-brick vaulting.

➕ 200 C4 ✉ ul. Starowiślna 15a
☎ 012 432 4550; www.donimirski.com

Where to...
Eat and Drink

Prices
Expect to pay for a three-course meal for one, excluding drinks:
€ under 50PLN   €€ 50PLN–100PLN   €€€ over 100PLN

Balaton €
The ambience of the two vaulted dining rooms of this Hungarian restaurant takes diners right back to the dog-eared days of communism, but despite the somewhat basic interior the food is outstanding, the service genuinely welcoming and prices low. The potato pancakes in Hungarian goulash are a rich and satisfying dream, as are the Tokaj wines. The menu is available in English as well as in Polish and Hungarian.

➕ 200 B4 ⊠ ul. Grodzka 37 ☎ 012 422 0469 ◉ Daily noon–10

Bar Smak €
Join the locals at long wooden benches for some filling Polish fare at this super cheap and simple lunch and dinner spot. It's also a good place to strike up a conversation over a few inexpensive beers in the evening.

➕ 200 A5 ⊠ ul Karmelicka 10 ☎ 012 431 2149 ◉ Daily 11–10

Chimera €€
Chimera comprises two neighbouring establishments – one a traditional Polish restaurant, the other a self-service salad bar

that has become a Krakowian institution, especially popular with students and vegetarians.

➕ 200 A4 ⊠ ul. Św. Anny 3 ☎ 012 292 1212; www.chimera.com.pl ◉ Daily noon–last customer

Dawno Temu na Kazimierzu €€
Cleverly disguised as four old shop fronts from the outside, this Jewish restaurant serving a simple menu of fowl and pierogi continues the theme inside with antique knick-knackery, sewing machines and even a carpenter's bench doubling up as a table. All this is designed to take diners back to the old Kazimierz, which it does remarkably well. Open on bank holidays when all other Kraków eateries are closed.

➕ 200 C3 ⊠ ul. Szeroka 1 ☎ 012 421 2117 ◉ Daily 10am–midnight

Gruzińskie Chaczapuri €
Not the most exciting of interiors but for those looking for something

a bit spicier after too many pierogi, the Georgian food (as in food from the former Soviet republic, not the US state) at this high-end fast food chain may hit the spot. Feast on large portions of seasoned grilled chicken, khachapuri (Georgian cheese pie), lavash (filled flatbread) and grilled pork washed down with remarkably good Georgian wines. The menu also features numerous vegetarian takes on khachapuri and lavash. Three other branches at ul. Sienna 4, ul. Św. Anny 4 and ul. Floriańska 26.

➕ 200 B4 ⊠ ul. Grodzka 3 ☎ 012 432 2600 ◉ Daily 11am–midnight

Miod Malina €€
A beautifully conceived folksy interior under sweeping arched vaulting meets diners at one of Kraków's best eateries, which could be described as a hybrid of Polish rural theme restaurant and Italian trattoria. The mix of Mediterranean and Eastern Europe works well, though both cuisines are kept

separate, no fusing here! Start with a hefty Polish soup, then move on to mains such as pasta or pizza and finish with trad Polish cheesecake.

🖩 200 B4 ⊠ ul. Grodzka 40 ☎ 012 430 0411 🕓 Daily noon–11

Nic Nowego €

More café-bar than classic pub, this British-owned venture is the best place to seek out in town if you are pining for a full English or some bona-fide "pub grub" such as chilli con carne. British footy on the box, English and Irish beers but stag night marauding kept to a minimum.

🖩 200 B4 ⊠ ul. Św. Kryża 15 ☎ 012 421 6188 🕓 Mon–Fri 7am–3am, Sat–Sun 10am–3am

Pod Krzyżykiem €€

Right on the market square, this restaurant dates back to the 16th century, and its name, "Under the Small Cross" refers to the old custom of marking drinking establishments with a small cross. Its extraordinary, quirky interior is entirely modern, however-, and complements the Polish cooking with a creative twist – dishes include salmon in green pepper sauce and roast duck with apple mousse. Eat outdoors in summer.

🖩 200 B4 ⊠ Rynek Główny 39 ☎ 012 433 7010; www.podkrzyzykiem.com 🕓 Daily noon–last customer

Pod Wawelem €€

The "Under Wawel" provides an authentically raucous beer hall atmosphere with monster portions of meat and veg served on wooden boards, barely hoistable steins of lager and a Bavarian-style oompah band. Reminiscent of Prague's Schweik theme pubs.

🖩 200 B3 ⊠ ul. Św Gertrudy 26/29 ☎ 012 421 2336 🕓 Daily 6:30am–midnight

Polskie Jadło Folwark €€

With a menu inspired by the 19th-century Polish manor house and a chunky rural interior, Folwark is the place to go for traditional Polish rural fare but with a slightly more refined adaptation. Typically filling Polish soups, bread-crumbed wild boar steak and beef sirloin are the dishes to look for and for dessert the cheesecake cannot be bettered.

🖩 200 B4 ⊠ ul. św. Kryża 13 ☎ 012 433 9785 🕓 Daily noon–11

Smak Ukraiński €

This great little Ukrainian restaurant occupies a cellar space and pleasant walled summer garden in quiet Kanonicza Street to the south of Rynek Główny. You'll find Polish and Ukrainian food have much in common and pierogi, borscht, shashlyk (kebabs), Kiev-style meat balls and kwas (a refreshing drink made from fermented black bread) are brought to your table by waiters in Ukrainian traditional apparel.

🖩 200 B3 ⊠ ul. Kanonicza 15 ☎ 012 421 9294 🕓 Daily noon–10

Wierzynek €€€

Claiming to have served top-notch grub to the world's high and mighty since medieval times, the Wierzynek on Kraków's centrepiece square remains as top-notch as it was when King Kazimir the Great entertained the crowned heads of Europe here in 1364. The mixed menu of traditional Polish and haute-cuisine dishes will certainly keep the tastebuds happy but dining here is not for those on any kind of budget.

🖩 200 B4 ⊠ Rynek Główny 15 ☎ 012 424 9600 🕓 Daily 1–midnight

Vega €

For some this is Kraków's best vegetarian restaurant (no hidden ham here) where the focus is firmly on cheap, tasty meat-free dishes served in a simple, candlelit dining space with large windows looking out onto the Planty. Ask waitresses to heap your plate high with veggie lasagne, pancakes, pierogi, rice, bigos and zapiekanki, all washed down with soya milk or herb tea.

🖩 200 B3 ⊠ ul. Św Gertrudy 7 ☎ 012 422 3494 🕓 Daily 9–9

Where to... Shop

Shopping has come a long way in Krakow since socialist times, especially since the arrival of the colossal Galeria Krakowska shopping mall in the city centre. As the country's main tourist hotspot, Krakow remains the best place in the land to pick up souvenirs of all kinds as well as mouth-watering local sweets and intriguing art and antiques.

SOUVENIRS

One of the best places in Poland to buy souvenirs is the covered internal street in the Sukiennice (▶ 81–82). The bustling thoroughfare is lined with stalls selling anything from genuine Baltic amber to made-in-China "I Love Poland" T-shirts and hand-carved chess sets to life-size portraits of Pope John Paul II. There's nowhere else in the country like it.

SHOPPING MALLS

Galeria Krakowska

With 270 retail outlets, this brand-new glimmering glass-and-steel edifice linked to the bus and main railway stations is Poland's largest shopping centre. All the facilities you would expect are available, though don't expect too many bargains in the shops. The complex also includes the Andels Hotel (▶ 92) and a much needed city-centre car park for 1,400 vehicles. (www.galeria-krakowska.pl).

Galeria Kazimierz

The smaller Kazimierz shopping mall (www.galeriakazimierz.pl) with 130 shops is perhaps slightly more upmarket despite boasting a branch of C&A. After a serious dose of retail therapy head for one of the on-site restaurants or spend an evening at the 10-screen cinema. Located to the east of the Jewish cemetery in the Kazimierz district and accessed by free bus from the city centre.

CONFECTIONARY AND *OBWARZANKI*

Regarded as the traditional confectionary of Krakow, Mieszanka Krakowska is fruit-flavour jelly covered in a layer of rich dark chocolate. The best place to buy it is the Wawel factory shop (Rynek Główny 33) where you can also pick up other chocolates and sweets bearing the local Wawel logo. Next door to Delicatesy, which stocks all sorts of edible Polish delicacies as well as more everyday food. At various strategic points around the city centre you're bound to notice small mobile stalls usually manned by elderly women selling what look like fat pretzel rings. These are *obwarzanki* (singular *obwarzanek*), white dough twisted into a ring and baked with poppy seeds, sea salt and occasionally other flavourings such as tomato and onion. They are softer than pretzels, harder than bagels and make a perfect budget mid-morning snack for just 1.20PLN.

ART

Galeria AG (Pl. Dominikański 2) and Galeria Osobliwości Este (ul. Sławkowska 16) are the finest places in Krakow to view and buy Polish art. Galeria Osobliwości Este in particular has a fascinating range of paintings, decorative items, furniture and exotic articles from Africa and Australasia. If you're in Kazimierz, Galerie d'Art Naif (ul. Józefa 11) is owned by one of Poland's greatest specialists in naive art, Leszek Macak.

Where to...
Be Entertained

As a tourist hotspot and cultural capital, Kraków hosts some of the best music, theatre, opera and art events in Poland. You'll be spoiled for choice as you trawl through reams of listings for Jewish and gypsy music concerts, folk events, piano recitals, church organ concerts, opera performances and even international sea shanty festivals.

CLASSICAL MUSIC AND OPERA

Classical music is provided by the **Kraków Philharmonic Orchestra** at the Philharmonic Hall (ul. Zwierzyniecka 1, www.filharmonia. krakow.pl). Performances usually take place on Friday and Saturday evenings. Opera can be enjoyed at a brand new, purpose-built opera venue at ul. Lubicz 48, home to the **Kraków Opera** (www.opera.krakow.pl).

FESTIVALS

Every month sees one festival or another fill Kraków's streets and/or entertainment venues. The biggest bash of the year is the **International Festival of Jewish Culture** in June, a week of music, lectures, readings, culinary events and general merriment in venues across Kazimierz (www.jewishfest.ival. pl). Other annual events you may catch are the **Kraków Marathon** (May), **Kraków City Festival** (June), the **Summer Jazz Festival**, **International Street Theatre**

Festival, and the **Crossroads Festival of Folk Music** (all July). August to October is the time for classical music, opera and early music festivals and December sees a Christmas market in Rynek Główny.

JAZZ

Kraków has at least eight establishments that describe themselves as jazz clubs. Pick of the bunch are **Boogie** (ul. Szpitalna 9), **U Muniaka** (ul. Floriańska 3) and **PiecArt** (ul. Szewska 12).

CITY TOURS

Contact the following companies for imaginative city tours: **Jarden** (Jewish tours, www.jarden.pl); **Communism Tours** (Nowa Huta, Socialist-era Kraków, www.crazyguides.com); **Kraków Tours** (Kraków walks, Wieliczka, Auschwitz, www.krakow-tours. com); **Orbis** (comprehensive range, www.orbis.krakow.pl); **Kraków**

Tourist Service (tailor-made trips, www.krakow-travel.com).

NIGHTCLUBS

Kraków boasts one of the most vibrant nightlife scenes in central Europe, thanks to the large student population and, in part, to the many stag parties which descend on the city. Clubs range from grungy beer-stained student joints to sleek VIP party venues with bouncers and cocktails.

WHAT'S ON

The *In Your Pocket guide to Kraków* (published six times annually) provides a sometimes tongue-in-cheek lowdown on cultural events, nightclubs and much besides. The much more highbrow *Karnet* (also published six times annually) is packed with detailed listings, reviews and information on every kind of cultural event happening in the city.

Małopolska and the Carpathians

Getting Your Bearings

Małopolska, which means "Little Poland", is anything but small and is, in fact, the name given to the entire southeastern quarter of the country. Overlooked by many tourists religiously following the Gdańsk-Warsaw-Kraków corridor, the delights of rural eastern Małopolska remain firmly off the beaten track and even an architectural gem such as Zamość receives fewer visitors than it deserves. Małopolska is divided from neighbouring Slovakia to the south by the mass of the Carpathian Mountains, a firm regional favourite for skiing and hiking.

From the bucolic countryside approaching the Ukrainian border to the international crowds at the Wieliczka salt mines, and from the horrors of Auschwitz to the carefree après-ski of night-time Zakopane, this chunk of Poland has many faces. Some come to enjoy the outdoor thrills offered by the Tatra Mountains, the best location for winter skiing and summer alpine hiking not only in Poland but all of central Europe, bar Austria. Others come as pilgrims to the Jasna Góra Monastery in Częstochowa to catch a glimpse of the Black Madonna, a miracle-working painting. Lublin is one of Poland's under-appreciated historical gems while Zamość prides itself on a UNESCO listing as a World Cultural Heritage Site, and Kazimierz Dolny is an increasingly popular destination. Nor is the region short of castles with magnificent examples in Lublin, Łancut and Baranów Sandomierski vying for attention. It's often said that places have something for everyone – Małopolska and the Carpathians truly do.

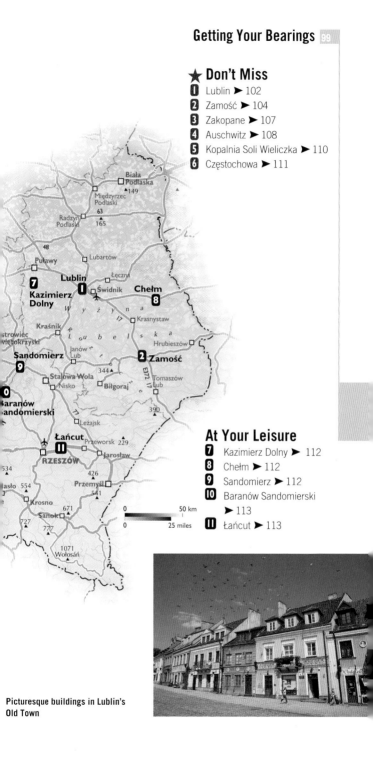

Biała Podlaska
▲149
Międzyrzec Podlaski
Radzyń Podlaski
63
165
48
Puławy
Lubartów
Lublin
Łęczna
7
Kazimierz Dolny
Świdnik
Chełm
8
W   y   ż   y   n   a
Kraśnik
Krasnystaw
strowiec iętokrzyski
L   u   b   e   l   s   k   a
Janów Lub
Hrubieszów
Sandomierz
9
344▲
2 Zamość
Stalowa Wola
Nisko
Biłgoraj
E372
Tomaszów Lub
0
aranów andomierski
390
Leżajsk
Łańcut
Przeworsk 229
11
RZESZÓW
Jarosław
426
534
Przemyśl
asło 554
541
Krosno
671
Sanok
727   777
1071 Wołosań

0 _____ 50 km
0 _____ 25 miles

Picturesque buildings in Lublin's Old Town

In Four Days

If you're not quite sure where to begin your travels, this itinerary recommends a practical and enjoyable four days in Małopolska and the Carpathians, taking in some of the best places to see using the Getting Your Bearings map on the previous page. For more information see the main entries.

Day One

Morning
Beginning in **1 Lublin** (► 102–103), start the day with a coffee and Polish doughnuts on ul. Grodzka at the heart of the Old Town. After soaking up the atmosphere of the old cobbled lanes and streets of the centre, move on to the castle museum and the frescoes at the Chapel of the Holy Trinity before dining at the excellent U Biesów.

Afternoon and Evening
Take a bus or drive the 50km (31 miles) east to see the chalk tunnels at **8 Chełm** (► 112) before heading south to the Renaissance pearl of Poland, Zamość, where you'll arrive just in time for supper in one of the main square's subterranean eateries. Walk off your meal with a tour of the sights illuminated against the night sky.

Day Two

Morning and Afternoon
Having overnighted in **2 Zamość** (► 104–106), a quick tour of the excellent Zamoyski Museum is a post-breakfast must before hitting the road again, Kraków bound, but with possible stops in **9 Sandomierz** (► 112–113) and **10 Baranów Sandomierski** (► 113) along the way.

Evening
Enjoy a dinner at one of Kraków's world-class restaurants before turning in.

Day Three

Morning
The short hop to ⑤ **Wieliczka** (► 110) to delve deep underground into the salt mines will have you up bright and early. Grab a bite to eat at the curious pit-bottom milk bar before travelling back west to ④ **Auschwitz** (► 108–109).

Afternoon and Evening
A sobering afternoon at the former death camp will leave you in contemplative mood. A low-key restaurant or classical music concert may be more suitable entertainment than a night on the tiles this evening.

Day Four

Morning and Afternoon
It is just possible in a long day-trip to visit the Jasna Góra Monastery in ⑥ **Częstochowa** (► 111), especially with your own transport. Remember that the miraculous picture is only revealed at certain times of the day so plan ahead. Alternatively, spend the day in ③ **Zakopane** (► 107) admiring the architecture or swishing down the pistes.

Evening
It's back to Kraków in the knowledge that you've had the full-blown Małopolska and Carpathians experience.

O Lublin

Despite its status as an important regional centre with an eventful history behind it, the city of Lublin 110km (68 miles) southeast of Warsaw is often overlooked by visitors sticking to the Gdańsk-Warsaw-Kraków corridor. This makes the city's atmospheric old town one of the country's best-kept secrets.

Old Town

Lublin's old historical core is, bar a couple of blocks, completely renovated and has been returned to its former glory. The main thoroughfare through the Old Town is the gently curving and undulating **ul. Grodzka**, which has a more authentic feel than many of Poland's re-established stars. The street runs from the 14th-century **Kraków Gate** to the **Grodzka Gate** near the castle, virtually the only remnants of the medieval town walls. Halfway along you arrive at the irregular-shaped **Rynek** which is dominated by the **Old Town Hall** dating from the 14th century but given a neoclassical makeover in 1781. Old lanes peel off ul. Grodzka and have a refreshingly uncommercial character.

Castle

Rising regally above oval-shaped plac Zamkowy, Lublin's castle sits atop a grassy mound like a giant sugar cube and is linked to ul. Grodzka by a raised balustraded walkway. This is no ancient pile, built as it was in the neo-Gothic style in the 1820s on the site of a 14th-century fortress. The facade facing the old town is a magnificent sight but seen from the sides the structure is far less impressive. It's now home to a large **museum**, which displays collections of Polish painting, folk art, coins, medals and period weapons. However, the highlight of the interiors is the **Chapel of the Holy Trinity** (Kaplica św. Trójcy). Here you will find precious medieval frescoes dating from the early 13th century and, in an effort to preserve them, entrance is limited to 25 visitors at a time.

Other Attractions

Just outside of the confines of the former city walls stands Lublin's impressive 16th-century **cathedral**, whose facade is dominated by six huge neoclassical columns. Inside you'll

---

LUBLIN: INSIDE INFO

In more depth Ul. Krakowskie Przedmieście is a wide, busy, shop-, café- and monument-lined thoroughfare extending from the Kraków Gate west to the Saxon Gardens, a stretch of verdant parkland and an ideal spot for shaking out the picnic blanket.

discover one of Poland's most ornate cathedral interiors, where almost every surface is decorated with frescoes. The adjoining tower can be climbed for views across the Old Town.

Lublin has its very own **open-air museum**, a small gathering of farmsteads located around 4km (2.5 miles) north of the centre. The city once had a thriving community of Jews, many of whom were killed in the nearby **Majdanek concentration camp** 4km (2.5 miles) southeast of the city centre. Wander around the barracks, museum and mausoleum to discover the story of this shocking place.

TAKING A BREAK

Magia (ul. Grodzka 2) attracts a young crowd as does **Złoty Osioł** (ul. Grodzka 5a). The **Ulice Miasta** restaurant, next to the Kraków Gate, where the interior is designed to look like exterior facades, is another option (▶ 116).

✚ 193 D3

Castle Museum
✉ ul. Zamkowa 9 ☎ 081 532 5001; www.zamek.lublin.pl 🕐 Jun–Aug Tue–Sat 10–5, Sun 10–6; Sep–May Tue, Thu–Sat 9–4, Wed, Sun 9–5 💰 Moderate

Open-air Museum
✉ al. Warszawksa 96 ☎ 081 533 3051; www.skansen.lublin.pl 🕐 Apr, Oct daily 9–5; May–Sep daily 10–6; Nov–Dec Sat–Mon 9–3 💰 Moderate

Majdanek
✉ Droga Męczenników Majdanka 67 ☎ 081 744 2640; www.majdanek.pl 🕐 Tue–Sun 8–4 💰 Free ❓ No children under 14

Lublin Castle's neo-Gothic facade is an impressive sight

② Zamość

Built from scratch in the late 16th century by nobleman Jan Zamoyski, no other town in Poland can match Zamość for Renaissance splendour. Ringed by red-brick defensive walls and earthworks, the town centre is one of the finest and best preserved examples of Renaissance urban planning in Europe and an architectural wonder. With more than 100 listed buildings and national monuments, Zamość was added to UNESCO's list of World Heritage Sites in 1992.

A Little History

Inspired by his student days spent at Padua University, Jan Zamoyski employed Italian architect Bernardo Morando to create a Renaissance urban masterpiece near to his birthplace. This was later surrounded by sturdy fortifications, first tested by the "Swedish Deluge" of the 17th century which they successfully held at bay. Merchants from all over Europe were drawn to the town thanks to its location on major trans-European trade routes and Zamość grew prosperous. Under the partitions of the late 18th century, Zamość eventually fell to the Russians whose insensitive alterations ruined many of the town's architectural gems. Despite witnessing fierce fighting during the Polish-Russian war of 1919–20 and liberation from the Nazis by the Red Army in 1945, Zamość survived almost intact and today is spared the worst excesses of mass tourism thanks to its slightly out-of-the-way location.

Above: The Renaissance architecture of the Town Hall dominates Rynek Wielki

Bottom left: Traditional arcaded town houses

Rynek Wielki

The centrepiece of the historical core is Rynek Wielki (Great Marketplace), a striking piazza measuring exactly 100m by 100m (110 by 110 yards) in the best traditions of Renaissance symmetry. In summer the flagstones and cobbles are awash with visitors and street cafés and this is also a natural venue for local events and celebrations. Three sides of the square are lined with unbroken arcading, which hides intricately carved doorways, entrances, vaulted hallways, shops and cafés. Above the arcading rise tall town houses, each sporting a new plaque with information in Polish and English on the history of the building, the builder and the first occupants. House No 25, the so-called **Kamienica Morando**, is where the town's architect himself lived and worked. The only break in the arcading is occupied by the impressive **town hall** with its pink and white façades, clock tower and double flights of steps, a later baroque addition, which sweep confidently up to the entrance. The tourist office is located in the right-hand corner of the building. To the right of the town hall, the excellent **Zamojski Museum** fills two town houses with exhibits on the history of the town including a scale model of

---

ZAMOŚĆ: INSIDE INFO

Hidden gem Check out the town's indoor market (Hala Targowa) housed in a former bastion by the Lvov Gate, although more interesting for the historical interior than the goods on sale.

In more detail To appreciate the extent of the town's sturdy fortifications, walk north from ul. Partyzantów through the pleasant parkland that surrounds the old red-brick walls and earthworks.

Zamość at the turn of the 18th century (notice the now absent
turrets on all the houses and the extent of the city walls),
mock-ups of period interiors and portraits of the Zamoyskis.
There are also sections devoted to local folk costumes, Slavic
forts in the region and traditional ceramics, and the interior
of the building and the views it affords of the square are worth
the admission charge alone.

**There are a
number of
cellar bars and
restaurants off
Reynek Wielki**

Other Attractions
Those expecting the **Zamoyski Palace** to the west of the
Rynek to be a grand Renaissance affair will be let down by the
rather drab official-looking building which now houses town
council offices and is closed to tourists. It lost its palatial looks
in the early 19th century when it was converted into a military
hospital by the Russians during their rule over this chunk
of Poland. However, the 16th-century **cathedral** across the
road makes up for the disappointment with its Renaissance
vaulting, stuccowork and rococo altar. Jan Zamoyski himself
is buried here in the family chapel. Behind the cathedral is
a small **Sacral Museum** housing a collection of religious
artwork.

Two of the original gates into the town have survived; the
Lviv Gate still stands next to the most frequented entrance
into the town, while, in contrast, the **Old Lublin Gate** near
the palace was only used as such for a short period after it was
built. The carefully planned grid of streets which seem to hold
the Rynek like a fly in a spider's web are lined with low-key
shops and houses in varying states of repair.

TAKING A BREAK
Zamość's Rynek Wielki has several cafés and bars (many of
which are situated underground). **The Blue Club** at No 4,
La Cantina U Włocha at No 6, **Art Jazz Cafe** at No 2 and
the **Chocolaterie** at No 3 are all accustomed to receiving
foreign visitors and have English menus.

✚ 193 E2

Zamojski Museum
✉ ul. Ormiańska 30 ☎ 084 638 6494; www.muzeum-zamojskie.one.pl
🕐 Tue–Sun 9–4 💷 Inexpensive

3 Zakopane

Poland's top alpine resort attracts more than 1.5 million tourists a year, most of whom come to ski or to use the town as a base from which to explore the surrounding countryside. Even if you haven't come to this area for the outdoor pursuits, the town is an interesting place to wander with some unusual architecture and museums.

The Willa Koliba is a perfect example of Zakopane architecture

Tatra Museum
The Muzeum Tatrzanskie, as it is called in Polish, features beautiful mock-ups of highlander cottage interiors, skilfully embroidered Tatra folk costumes, colourful traditional glass paintings and exhibits on notable individuals to whom Zakopane owes much for its current prosperity and popularity.

Museum of the Zakopane Style
Stanisław Witkiewicz was a gifted painter, writer, art critic and most importantly an architect who created the so-called Zakopane style of architecture inspired by the design of timber Górale houses in the Podhale region. This museum dedicated to Stanisław Witkiewicz and his creations is housed in the Willa Koliba, the first building erected in the style in the 1880s.

Zakopane's Architectural Gems
In addition to the buildings housing the above museums, other fine examples of the distinctive Zakopane style can be seen around town including the Willa Pod Jedłami in the Bystre district, the Church of the Holy Family on Krupówki Street and the chapel in the Jaszczurówka district. Witkiewicz's grave can be found at St Clement's church.

TAKING A BREAK
After a morning on the ski slopes or exploring Zakopane's museum's and timber pearls, head straight to the main **ul. Krupówki**, where you'll be spoiled for choice for lunch spots.

✚ 196 A1

Tatra Museum
✉ ul. Krupówki 10 ☎ 018 201 5205; www.muzeumtatrzanskie.com.pl
🕐 Tue–Sat 9–5, Sun 9–3. Closed Mon–Tue in winter 💰 Moderate

Museum of the Zakopane Style
✉ ul. Kościeliska 18 ☎ 018 201 3602 🕐 Wed–Sat 9–5, Sun 9–3
💰 Moderate

4 Auschwitz

You may not have heard of the small town of Oświęcim but you will certainly know it by the more infamous German name of Auschwitz. Not much had ever happened in this sleepy corner of Poland until 1940 when the Nazis located a prison for political prisoners, POWs and common criminals on the outskirts.

Following the Wannsee conference of 1942, where the Nazis' decided on their so-called "final solution" for the Jews, Auschwitz was extended and Birkenau, another camp nearby originally intended for Soviet POWs, was completed on a huge scale. This would become the largest death camp in occupied Europe and a place synonymous with the horror, suffering and inhumanity of the Holocaust. Liberated by the Red Army in 1945, the camp remains largely as they found it and is now a museum that relates the stories of the more than a million people murdered here.

The Museum

The self-guided tour begins at the visitor centre, where you can buy a plan of the camp, watch a film on the camp and get your bearings. Enter the complex via a gate above which the infamous slogan "Arbeit macht frei" ("Work brings freedom") once mocked all who passed through. The original prison blocks, which belonged to the first prison built here immediately after the Nazi invasion, are your first stop. Six blocks can be entered, each containing harrowing photographs, documents and other exhibits that bring home in a powerful but far from gory way just what happened here. Most thought-provoking are the mountains of personal effects confiscated from prisoners (artificial limbs, suitcases, spectacles, shoes, brushes, pots and pans) and transported

Roll call booth in Oświęcim

AUSCHWITZ: INSIDE INFO

Top tip Be sure to buy the essential 24-page booklet (available in English) on sale at the museum, containing a map and explanations of all the exhibits in the camps.

One to miss The film shown every hour at the museum is not worth waiting for as the series of stills are the same as those you will see in the camps themselves and even the commentary is similar to the text in the above-mentioned booklet.

Auschwitz I exhibition entitled Extermination in Oświęcim

back to Germany for the Nazi war effort. These plus a field of human hair, a mound of dentures, children's shoes and many other items survived despite the guards' attempts to burn the evidence of their crimes as the Red Army advanced. The tour then continues to the Death Block (block 11), where prisoners were flogged and executed in the yard outside, and the Assembly Square where the morning roll call and summary executions were performed. The next section of the exhibition is dedicated to the various nationalities imprisoned here.

Auschwitz II-Birkenau

From Auschwitz I it's a 3km (2-mile) walk or short shuttle bus ride to Auschwitz II-Birkenau. In some ways the sheer scale of the camp, where around a fifth of the buildings have survived, makes Birkenau more powerful than Auschwitz I. Visitors enter along the infamous railway tracks, which pass through the red-brick gates and split the camp in half. The watchtower above is a good vantage point from which to get an idea of the size of the camp before heading off to view the wooden cattlesheds, which held 400 prisoners, and the remains of the gas chambers where prisoners were murdered using Zyklon B gas. At the end of the railway tracks there is a Communist-era monument to the victims of Auschwitz in 20 languages.

TAKING A BREAK

The welcome **milk bar** by the entrance to the museum is where everyone heads for refreshment. It serves Polish favourites as well as pizza, chips and hamburgers.

195 F2 ☒ ul. Więźniów Oświęcimia 20 ☎ 033 843 2022; www.auschwitz.org.pl ⏰ Summer daily 8–7, shorter hours in winter 🎫 Free

5 Kopalnia Soli Wieliczka

Easily the most popular half-day trip out of Kraków is to the UNESCO-listed Wieliczka Salt Mine just outside the city limits and reachable by train and bus. Burrowed as deep as 327m (1,073 feet) into the salt deposits are an incredible 300km (186 miles) of corridors, shafts and halls, the highlight of which is a subterranean church carved entirely out of salt.

Billed as the longest continuously worked mine in the world, the precious and once highly valuable commodity has been extracted from Wieliczka's tunnels for more than 700 years. The 90-minute tour starts with a seemingly endless descent which take visitors deep into the innards of the mine. Visitors tour the three upper levels of the mine and the route takes in various halls, underground lakes, salt statues, mining machinery and mock-ups of mining scenes showing the harsh environment the miners had to endure. One of the caverns is so large that an underground bungee jumping world record was set there. The real showstopper, though, comes in the form of an underground church, the **Chapel of the Blessed Kinga.** Everything you see here is salt (even the chandeliers are made from rare salt crystals) and it took 30 years of boring, chiseling, chipping and smoothing by early 20th-century miners to create this briny basilica. St Kinga's is a fully operational church with services taking place every Sunday morning and even subterranean marriage ceremonies.

TAKING A BREAK

At the end of your tour of the salt mine, take a welcome break at Poland's deepest restaurant, at the bottom of the mine.

➕ 196 A3 ✉ 10 Daniłowicza Street ☎ 012 278 7302; www.kopalnia.pl
🕒 Summer daily 7:30–7:30, winter 8–5 💰 Expensive

This incredible chapel is made entirely from salt, including the chandeliers

6 Częstochowa

The rather lacklustre town of Częstochowa would receive few visitors were it not for a single painting kept in the local Jasna Góra Monastery. The miracle-working Black Madonna depicted with an infant Jesus attracts so many devout Catholics that the town is rated the fifth most popular place of pilgrimage on earth after Varanasi, Mecca, Lourdes and the Vatican.

The elaborate basilica in the Jasna Góra Monastery

The monastery sits high on a hill at the western end of long and arrow-straight Al. Najśswiętszej Marii Panny (Al. NMP to its friends) and dominates the town in many ways. It's not known exactly where the painting of the Black Madonna originated but the miracles attributed to it began to attract pilgrims as early as the 15th century. Its popularity increased after the picture was believed to have saved Poland from the Swedish invasion in the 1650s and continues to this day. The painting is kept in the ornate caroque Chapel of the Miraculous Picture (Kaplica Cudownego Obrazu) at the monastery, which is constantly busy with visitors.

The next-door basilica is similarly ornate and the monastery also has its own museum where visitors can see period weapons, exhibitions on the Solidarity Movement, Lech Wałęsa's Nobel Peace Prize and replicas of the Miraculous Picture.

The treasury is also worth a look around for its hundreds of rosaries, crucifixes, chalices and pieces of jewellery dedicated to the monastery over the centuries and now housed in chunky oak display cases.

TAKING A BREAK

The best place to head for coffee or a light lunch is Al. NMP which cuts the town in two. **Mithos**, an ice cream parlour at No. 61, **Caffe Milano** at No 59 and small and chintzy **Secesja** at No 50 are the pick of the bunch. In the summer months there are refreshment stands and kiosks set up near the entrance to the monastery.

🕂 195 E3 ✉ ul. O. A. Kordeckiego 2 ☎ 034 377 7777;
www.jasnagora.pl ⏰ Daily 5:30–9; the painting is only revealed from 6am until noon then at least once in the afternoon at either 1pm, 2pm or 3pm
💶 Free

At Your Leisure

7 Kazimierz Dolny

This tiny town around 40km (25 miles) west of Lublin is one of the prettiest in the region, luring artists, filmmakers and tourists to its wealth of authentic old architecture nestled between two hills by the wide-flowing Vistula. The old core is centred around the Rynek, which has a covered wooden well in the middle and is lined with a mixed bag of architectural gems of all shapes and sizes. Low wooden shacks stand side-by-side with magnificent Renaissance town houses and the scene is watched over by a dinky Gothic parish church which sports much Renaissance cladding. The Rynek radiates streets and lanes in all directions and here you will

Kazimierz Dolny from the castle ruins

come across other attractions such as a Museum of Goldsmithery (ul. Zamkowa 2) and the Local History Museum (ul. Senatorska 11). You can also admire some superb views of Kazimierz Dolny from the top of the Mountain of Three Crosses as well as from the watchtower, once part of the town's defences.

➕ 192 C3
Tourist Information Centre
✉ Rynek 27 ☎ 081 881 0046 🕐 Summer 8–5:30, winter 8–4, shorter hours at weekends

8 Chełm

Just short of the Ukrainian border, Chełm (pronounced *khewm*) was built on an 800m-thick (2,600ft) deposit of chalk, and it's the system of dusty tunnels carved out beneath the old centre that attracts visitors today. The world's only underground chalk mine (Zabytkowa Kopalnia Kredy) once extended for over 12km (7.5 miles), until the town began to suffer from subsidence and the tunnels were filled in. Just under 2km (1 mile) of safe passageways were left as a tourist attraction so the town continues to thrive economically from its chalky setting. To see the tunnels you have to join a 45-minute guided Polish-language tour. In addition to its subterranean delights, Chełm also boasts a pair of impressive churches and a large museum.

➕ 193 E3
Tourist Information Centre
✉ ul. Lubelska 63 ☎ 082 565 3667 🕐 Summer 8–5, winter 8–4, shorter hours at weekends

Chełm Chalk Tunnels
✉ ul. Lubelska 55a
☎ 082 565 2530;
www.zabytkowakopalniakredy. cob.pl 🕐 Tours at 11, 1, 4 💰 Moderate

9 Sandomierz

A mix of old architecture, two engaging museums and a handful of noteworthy churches make Sandomierz an interesting stopping-off point or a place to base yourself to explore the Sandomierz Valley. Sandomierz's epicentre is the Rynek in the middle of which stands its most famous and oldest building, the Gothic and Renaissance town hall, which now houses one branch of the Regional Museum. Another branch is located in the castle some 300m (327 yards) to the south along ul. Zamkowa. Just to the east of the castle, the Church of St James dating from the late 12th century is often cited as the first brick-built place of worship in Poland. Like Chełm, Sandomierz also has an underground side, this time wine and grain cellars hewn out of soft rock. Visitors have access to just 500m (545 yards) of tunnels (entrance off the Rynek) and guided tours leave hourly.

➕ 192 B2
Tourist Information Office
➕ ul. Rynek 12 ☎ 015 832 3088

Baranów Sandomierski castle has beautiful Renaissance arcading

🔟 Baranów Sandomierski

The castle on the edge of this small town is one of Poland's finest Renaissance buildings and worth a detour. Designed in the late 16th century for the Leszczyński family by an Italian architect, the courtyard around which the palace is built is as perfect an example of Renaissance arcading as you will find anywhere and has earned it the nickname – "Little Wawel". The ground floor is packed full of period furniture and décor, and down in the basement a museum hosts temporary shows. Interestingly, a small section of the castle is home to a modern hotel.

➕ 197 D4
Castle
✉ ul. Zamkowa 20 ☎ 015 811 8039; www.baranow.com.pl ⏰ Summer Tue–Sun 9–7, winter 9–4

🔟 Łańcut

The small town of Łańcut is most famous for its huge castle, one of the best in all Poland. The original building dates from the 17th century but has been lost under several rebuilds and renovations. The neo-baroque facade visitors admire today dates from the late 19th century, but the real joy of Łańcut castle is its interiors packed to the rafters with precious works of art. There's also an orangery and a carriage museum. You can end your visit with a relaxing stroll in the parkland which surrounds the castle. Tours, which take in around 50 rooms, are guided and last approximately 90 minutes.

➕ 197 E3
Castle
✉ ul. Zamkowa 1 ☎ 017 225 2008; www.zamek-lancut.pl ⏰ Generally 10–4; shorter hours Mon

The neo-baroque facade of Łańcut Castle

Where to... Stay

Prices

Expect to pay per night for a double room (in peak season):

€ under 200PLN   €€ 200PLN–500PLN   €€€ over 500PLN

Hotel Galicja €€

Few stay over in Auschwitz, most treating the town as a day trip from Kraków. If you do decide to sleep here, then arguably the best hotel in town is the three-star Galicja located in the centre of the town proper around 3km (2 miles) from the Auschwitz camp museum. Standard double rooms are well equipped but a touch on the snug side for two people. The hotel management are proud of the fact that Boney M and President Chirac have stayed here since it opened, the mention of which will have you humming *Daddy Cool* over dinner in one of the three hotel eateries

🔲 195 F2 🔯 ul. Dąbrowskiego 119 🔯 033 843 6115; www.hotelgalicja.com.pl

Sekwana €

If you're going to stay in Częstochowa, you might as well do it as near to Jasna Góra as you can, and Sekwana at the bottom of the hill is about as close as you'll get. This cosy 60-bed establishment is comfortable enough for a night or two and has a sound restaurant. Rooms are no interior decorator's dream but they do the job.

🔲 195 E3 🔯 Wieluńska 24 🔯 034 324 6367; www.sekwana.pl (Polish only)

Grand Lublinianka €€€

It doesn't get better than this in southeastern Poland. Situated conveniently near to the shops on ul. Krakowskie Przedmieście and the historical centre, the 72-room, four-star Lublinianka packs in the style and guestrooms are spacious. Lublin's top sleep also boasts the chic and pricey Bel Etage restaurant, mezzanine cigar bar and a ritzy cafe.

🔲 193 D3 🔯 ul. Krakowskie Przedmieście 56 🔯 081 446 6100; www.lublinianka.com

Sabala €€

You won't go wrong with this three-star Sabala located in a late 19th-century timber building on the main drag through town. As you might expect, the timber continues on the inside with hefty exposed beams and pine panelling throughout the 58 comfortable guestrooms, the perfect place to return after a chilly day on the pistes. Chunky wooden beds, coarse highland blankets and traditional Górale furniture give the feel of a shepherd's cottage high in the mountains.

🔲 196 A1 🔯 ul. Krupówki 11 🔯 018 201 5092; www.sabala.zakopane.pl

Zamoyski €€

Choose one of the 54 rooms at this Orbis chain hotel, the best in town, to enjoy a prime location a few steps off the Rynek. Housed in a series of conjoined, modernised town houses next door to the town hall, some rooms have views of the square. Service is polite, facilities well run and there are two reliable restaurants on the premises.

🔲 193 E2 🔯 ul. Kołłątaja 2–6 🔯 084 639 2516; www.orbis.pl

Where to...
Eat and Drink

Prices
Expect to pay for a three-course meal for one, excluding drinks:

€ under 50PLN   €€ 50PLN–100PLN   €€€ over 100PLN

AUSCHWITZ

Menada €€
Established very solidly with the thousands of international visitors down the road at the Auschwitz camp museum in mind, this contemporary restaurant in a quiet residential district roughly half way between the railway station and the museum serves up an unexpected blend of Polish cuisine and international dishes ranging from tortillas to pasta to chicken curry. Going Polish may be the best policy as some of the other dishes may lack the spice they need to satisfy Western palates.

✚ 195 F2 ⊠ ul. Więźniów Oświęcimia 8 ☎ 033 844 5303 ⏰ Daily 11–11

CZĘSTOCHOWA

Karczma u Braci Kiemliczów €€
Częstochowa hardly teems with Michelin stars, fast feeds for pilgrims being more the order of the day, but this attempt at a rural theme restaurant, just a short walk away from the monastery is better than most. Stocky country-style fittings let you know what to expect – heavy Polish fare, just what you'll need after tussling with a thousand teenage pilgrims in order to get a fleeting glimpse of the Miraculous Picture.

✚ 192 C3 ⊠ ul. Witkiewicza 2 ☎ 081 881 0426 ⏰ Sun–Thu 9:30–midnight, Fri–Sat 9:30–2am

KAZIMIERZ DOLNY

U Fryzjera €
Inhabiting an old spit-and-sawdust barber's shop, the original U Fryzjera is a superb place to try some authentic Jewish fare while tapping your foot, on the exposed floorboards, along to the live *klezmer* bands that perform here. The extensive English menu is packed with a wealth of mouthwatering choices such as lamb stew and stuffed potato cakes as well as many special Jewish holiday foods which contain interesting combinations of ingredients. There is even a special children's menu, though the vegetarian options leave quite a bit to be desired.

✚ 195 E3 ⊠ ul. Wielunska 16 ☎ 034 372 6264 ⏰ Daily noon–10

LUBLIN

U Biesów €
The bijou U Biesów, occupying one downstairs vaulted room of a pretty Rynek-side town house, is an uncomplicated affair with basic candlelit dark-wood tables, bare tiled floors and wrought-iron chandeliers. Here the focus is most definitely on satisfying customers with polite but not overbearing service and authentic cuisine. The English menu features some interesting takes on Polish staples and this is a good a place as any to sample the local Perla beer. In summer, when the weather is warm, you can even savour your meal outside on the square.

✚ 193 D3 ⊠ Rynek 18 ☎ 081 532 1648 ⏰ Daily 10am–11pm

Ulice Miasta €

Making the inside of an eatery look like the outside is a more common theme in Poland than you might expect, but the "Streets of the Town" next to the Kraków Gate pulls it off particularly well. Over three levels the facades of various shops and businesses come equipped with street lighting, wrought-iron balconies and signs. The first floor is a gallery space with images of old Lublin, but all this shouldn't distract you from the well-prepared Polish food on offer, including several vegetarian choices.

⊞ 193 D3 ⊠ Plac Łokietka 3 ☎ 081 534 0592 ⊙ Sun–Thu 10am–11pm, Fri–Sat 10am–1am

ZAKOPANE

Mała Szwajcaria €€

If you've grown weary of mountains of meat and piles of *pierogi* and *karczmas* that resemble a cross between little Red Riding Hood's cottage and a junk shop, then let Little Switzerland return a little style into your life. Housed in an attractive timber building in the town centre, this upmarket restaurant with its crystal glasses and pressed linen tablecloths serves up a typically Swiss menu of raclette, fondue and Alpine meat dishes as well as Polish pancakes and soups. The chocolate fondue accompanied by a bottle from the extensive wine list makes a great après-ski experience.

⊞ 196 A1 ⊠ ul. Zamoyskiego ☎ 018 201 2076 ⊙ Mon–Thu 9–11, Fri–Sun 9–midnight

Pstrąg Górski €€

Located in the centre of town, the name of this restaurant translates as "mountain trout" and it's this dish which plays starring role on the menu. Enjoy this freshwater treat, meat dishes and other Polish standards served on huge wooden platters inside or out on the terrace by a trickling alpine stream.

⊞ 196 A1 ⊠ ul. Krupówki 6 ☎ 018 206 4163 ⊙ Daily 9am–10:30pm

Staro Izba €€

Though obviously not the real deal, wedged into a 19th-century town house, the "Old Room" is one of Poland's most enjoyable Tatra-style taverns, with an interior crammed with highlander knick-knackery and waitresses trussed up in traditional costume. Food often comes served on wooden boards instead of plates and the menu is an intensely meaty affair with what the owners claim are local dishes. Whatever you choose, wash it all down with Polish beer on tap or some "mountaineer's tea".

⊞ 196 A1 ⊠ ul. Krupówki 28 ☎ 018 201 3391 ⊙ Daily 11–last customer

ZAMOŚĆ

Muzealna €€

Accessed down a set of spiral steps burrowed into the square next to the museum, Zamość's best eatery resides in three deep, cosy brick cellars, each one decked out to look like a Renaissance dining hall complete with sturdy dark timber tables, high-backed chairs and heavy maroon drapes. Dishes consisting of all kinds of meat plus fish, *pierogi*, *naleśniki* and a choice of heavy soups come in absolutely monster portions, and there is a special kid's menu. For dessert try the blissfully calorific chocolate-filled pancakes. In summer you can eat outside on the terrace.

⊞ 193 E2 ⊠ ul. Ormiańska 30 ☎ 084 638 7300 ⊙ Daily 10am–11pm

Verona €€

Stylish café above ground, clean-cut New York Italian joint in the brick cellars down below, the Verona, with its modern menu of pasta and pizza, gurgling espresso machine, shiny black and red leather, swirling stucco and coffee-and-cream decor, is the perfect antidote to Poland's rather stodgy rural theme eateries. It also boasts the best stocked bar in town.

⊞ 193 E2 ⊠ Rynek Wielki 5 ☎ 084 638 9031 ⊙ Daily 11am–midnight

Where to... Shop

Kraków is, without doubt, the shopping hub of Małopolska and one of the best places in the country to buy souvenirs or browse gleaming Western-style shopping centres. Out in the countryside options are more limited, though Zakopane and Wieliczka do provide opportunities to buy some unique take-home items.

ANTIQUES, HANDICRAFTS & ARTWORK

Częstochowa has both a branch of **Cepelia** at Al. NMP 64 not far from the monastery and a large Desa antique emporium at Al. NMP 40. There are also several stalls around Jasna Góra selling religious items to pilgrims. There are further regional branches of Cepelia in Lublin

(ul. Krakowskie Przedmieście 22), Auschwitz (ul. Śniadeckiego 23), Sandomierz (ul. Opatowska 11) and Zamość (Rynek Wielki 11). With their Górale folk culture and traditions, the Tatra Mountains and Zakopane are *the* places to pick up highlander folk costumes, handicrafts and artwork and the town's market is a good source of interesting items as well as the more mundane. Kazimierz Dolny is well known for its varied galleries where local artists sell their creations and in summer numerous stalls sprout up selling local handicrafts as well as general souvenirs available in many other places.

HIGHLANDER CHEESE

Tatran cheese is sold across Poland but it's best bought at source in

Zakopane. The decorated cylinders of unpasteurised sheep and ewe's milk cheese are good to eat or to take home as a unique gift which would involve much searching to source at home. Oscypek is the best known though there are many other rarer types to be found.

GIFTS FROM WIELICZKA

Having emerged blinking from the high-speed lift from the bottom of the Wieliczka salt mine, you will find yourself, somewhat conveniently, in the large gift shop. Here you can purchase all manner of items with a salty theme – bath salts, carved salt crystals, salt lamps and even pieces of jewellery made of the stuff, as well as more widely available items such as maps, guides, chess sets, DVDs, mugs etc.

AUSCHWITZ

While souvenirs are, rather understandably, thin on the ground

in Auschwitz, the museum shop and a nearby kiosk do stock DVDs and various books on the history of the camp. Alternatively you can shop for a wide range of books, posters, CDs, DVDs and guidebooks online directly from the Auschwitz website (www.auschwitz.org.pl). No tourist trinket kiosks are permitted to set up shop near any of Poland's former concentration camps.

OUTDOOR EQUIPMENT

Zakopane has plenty of outdoor shops and specialist ski centres for those who have forgotten their walking poles or have left their ski gloves at home. Most of these can be found on ul. Krupowki and stock internationally popular brands as well as cheaper Polish alternatives. As in all major ski resorts, it's also possible to hire skis, boots and ski poles at several places in Zakopane and the hire rates are very reasonable.

Where to...
Be Entertained

In traditional rural Poland, folk festivals are the highlights of the cultural calendar and this region has some of the best. On the sporting front, skiing and hiking are big in the Tatra Mountains around Zakopane.

FESTIVALS

The colourful **Zakopane Festival of Mountain Folklore**, held every year in mid to late August in the village of Rownia Krupowa, is one of Poland's best folk festivals, attracting highlander people from many mountainous areas of Europe and around the world. The festival is a superb chance to sample highland cuisines and watch performances of traditional music and dance. Another big international folk event in Małopolska is **Eurofolk** held in Zamość every July or August which fills the Rynek with traditional song and dance performed by ensembles from places as far away as Sri Lanka and Chile. Another folk festival you may want to catch takes place in Kazimierz Dolny in late June under the title of the **Festival of Folk Bands and Singers**. As a major world pilgrimage destination, Częstochowa hosts so-called **Marian feasts** seven times a year, the most significant being the **Feast of the Assumption** on August 15th. However, unless you are a devout Catholic pilgrim, these are probably times to avoid.

MUSIC

The **Filharmonia Lubelska** based in Lublin (ul. Skłodowskiej-Curie 5; www.filharmonialubelska.pl [Polish only]) is one of the best in the country and has a wide-ranging repertoire which it performs at a large purpose-built concert hall. Zamość hosts no less than three popular **jazz festivals** in July (Jazz in the Borderlands), September (Jazz Vocalists Festival) and December (Blues Festival). Contact the Kosz Jazz Club (www.kosz.zam.pl) for further details.

SKIING AND HIKING

Zakopane is by far the largest winter sports destination in Poland and the biggest resort in the vicinity of the town is the **Nosal Ski Complex** (www.nosal.pl) with six ski lifts, one red slope and five green and learner slopes, restaurants and a ski hire centre. There's also a ski school for beginners and children. In late spring, summer and early autumn the Tatras, and to a lesser extent the Beskid Mountains, are blissful retreats for walkers, hikers and climbers. Zakopane is a frequent venue for ski jump competitions and other winter sports, even at the height of summer!

WHAT'S ON

As in all Poland's large cities and tourist/expat hotspots, the **In Your Pocket guides** provide a wealth of information and restaurant, bar, café and accommodation listings both online and in paper form. The only guide available for Małopolska and the Carpathians is the Zakopane version, though the Kraków guide also covers Wieliczka, Auschwitz and occasionally other locations in the Tatra foothills. Tourist information centres in individual towns and cities across the region also keep detailed timetables of all the events which are happening in their areas.

Silesia

Getting Your Bearings

Silesia, in the southwest corner of the country, is historically one of the most interesting and diverse regions of Poland and, in some ways, the least Polish of all the country's provinces. From the industrial Katowice conurbation to the bucolic scenery of the Karkonosze Mountains to the vibrant cultural offerings of Wrocław, the regional capital, Silesia cannot fail to captivate the visitor.

Silesia has had a turbulent past and to fully make sense of the region, visitors should be forearmed with at least an outline of its history. The 11th-century Silesian Piasts aligned themselves with Poland but later rulers turned to powerful Bohemian kings to the south. As part of Bohemia, Silesia automatically passed to the Austrian Empire when the Habsburgs gained power in the Czech lands in the early 17th century. They in turn lost the province to Prussia in the mid-17th-century War of Austrian Succession. Silesia only rejoined Poland in 1945 when the Germans were forced out. Influences left by this succession of rulers are evident in the architecture of the churches, art and museum exhibits.

The region is divided into Upper Silesia, the seldom-visited industrial heartlands, and Lower Silesia around Wrocław, the region's cultural and transport hub. City-breakers to Wrocław should consider escaping the confines of the city for a few days to hike in the Karkonozse Mountains or the Ziemia Kłodzka, to visit the churches and cathedrals in places like Nysa and Krzeszów or to take the waters at the spa in Kudowa Zdrój.

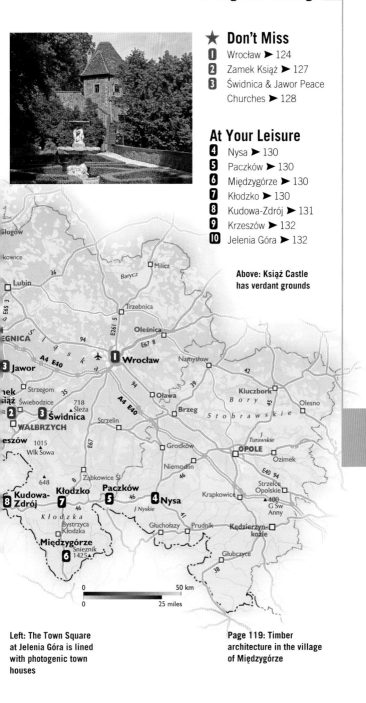

Above: Książ Castle has verdant grounds

Left: The Town Square at Jelenia Góra is lined with photogenic town houses

Page 119: Timber architecture in the village of Międzygórze

In Three Days

If you're not quite sure where to begin your travels, this itinerary recommends a practical and enjoyable three days in Silesia, taking in some of the best places to see using the Getting Your Bearings map on the previous page. For more information see the main entries.

Day 1

Morning
The vast majority of visitors to Silesia start their exploration in ❶ **Wrocław** (➤ 124–126) where your first stop should be the grand old Rynek. From there make your way into the streets of the old town to discover the city's Gothic churches and the baroque Aula Leopoldinum at the university. Refuel at one of the city centre's many outdoor cafés.

Afternoon and Evening
Spend an hour viewing the spectacular Racławice Panorama before crossing the River Odra (left) to view the churches and tranquil parkland around the cathedral. In the evening make sure you've booked a table at the superb Piwnica Świdnicka (➤ 135).

Day 2

Morning
Beat Wrocław's traffic jams by making an early start for the ❸ **Jawor** peace church before heading southeast to see its twin in ❸ **Świdnica** (right; ➤ 128–129). Grab a light lunch on the town's agreeable central square.

Afternoon and Evening
❷ **Zamek Książ** (top right; ➤ 127) is just a short drive from Świdnica and this should be your next destination. After exploring

the castle's rooms and surveying the surrounding landscape from the top of the tower either head back to the city or stay over at the Hotel Zamkowy to take an evening stroll in the castle grounds, more atmospheric once the tour buses have left.

Day 3

Morning
An hour's drive southeast from Książ will bring you to the Ziemia Kłodzka, where the town of **7 Kłodzko** (➤ 130) should be your first stop. Climb to the top of the hill for a scramble round the fortress before heading back down through the underground cellars to dine on the square at W Ratuszu restaurant (➤ 134).

Afternoon and Evening
In the afternoon head west to **8 Kudowa-Zdrój** (right; ➤ 131– 132) where you can soothe body and soul at the local spa or inspect the macabre Chapel of Skulls. Alternatively, enjoy some easy hiking around Międzygórze, perhaps climbing Śnieżnik, the highest peak in the Ziemia Kłodzka.

Wrocław

As Poland's fourth largest city, the capital of Polish Silesia and a major regional cultural centre with a history extending over 1,000 years, Wrocław is essential viewing for anyone exploring the southwest. Founded around AD1000 by Poland's earliest rulers, the city has endured some turbulent times with the Tatars, Czechs, Austrians, Prussians, Nazis and the Red Army all having left their mark, most notably the last two in the list, which reduced the city to rubble in the closing stages of World War II.

Rynek and Around

Few can fail to be impressed by Wrocław's main square, a centrepiece any city would be proud of. Towering five- and six-storey old burghers' town houses define a cobbled stage where the main players are the original red-brick Gothic **town hall** and its numerous appendages in a variety of architectural styles. It's hard to imagine that when the dust had settled on the liberation of Wrocław by the Soviets in 1945, most of the Rynek and the surrounding streets were left a smouldering heap of landfill. Part of the town hall now contains a **museum and gallery**, which not only provide the opportunity to view city treasures but also allow you to explore the renovated interiors. Adjacent to the main square lies smaller Plac Solny, the old salt market where sacks of the precious white stuff have been replaced by a 24-hour flower market.

Above: The Town Hall Clock Tower and the long café terraces make the Rynek an imposing main square

The Silesian capital is dotted with churches but the most impressive in the historical core must be the **Church of St Elizabeth**, to the northwest of the Rynek. This mountain of Gothic red brick is one of the oldest in the city and, although the interior is little to write home about, the views from the 90m (295-foot) spire are well worth the ascent. Another remarkable place of worship is the Church of St Vincent, near the university. It is the largest church in Wrocław, built on the site of a Romanesque rotunda but destroyed in 1945. It was rebuilt only in the 1990s. Also at the university you can admire the city's top piece of Habsburg-era baroque at the **Aula Leopoldinum**, a riot of stucco, cherubs, trompe l'oeil frescoes and religious imagery which fills a hall used for induction and graduation ceremonies that is often open to the public.

Racławice Panorama

Amid all its grand burghers' houses, Gothic churches and medieval cobbled squares, it may come as a surprise to learn that Wrocław's most popular tourist attraction is an unsightly 1980s circular concrete bunker around half a kilometre (547yds) east of the Rynek. However, all becomes clear when you enter and discover an amazing 360-degree canvas depicting the Battle of Racławice, painted by two Lvov artists in the late 19th century. The battle took place in 1794 between the insurrectionist forces of national hero, Tadeusz Kościuszko, and the Imperial Russian army. Despite Kościuszko's triumph, the Russians went ahead with the Third Partition of the country but the victory lived on in Polish folk memory. The painting, intended to remind patriotic Poles of their history, became history itself during and after World War II. Until 1944 it was on show in Lvov (now in Ukraine) but was damaged by a shell. Following Lvov's annexation by Stalin in 1945, many of the city's Polish residents moved to Wrocław, which had been emptied of Germans by forced repatriations. They brought the painting with them but imagery of a Polish victory over Russian troops was deemed too politically sensitive and it wasn't until 1980 that the panorama was put on display here (hence the ugly bunker). Visitors enter at given intervals, are issued with wireless headphones through which a soundtrack in English is transmitted, and follow the battle being played out across the sweeping canvas.

Top: Detail of the ornate gable of the Town Hall

Piasek and Tumski Islands

The islands formed by the River Odra to the north of the centre are home to a tranquil quarter of churches and Church administration buildings, which occupy the site of the first settlement. The obvious highlight here is the **Cathedral of St John the Baptist**, Wrocław's patron saint, completely obliterated during the war but painstakingly recreated with all its Gothic and baroque features restored. Climb the tower for

---

WROCŁAW: INSIDE INFO

Hidden gem Situated 3km (2 miles) to the east of the Rynek, Wrocław's UNESCO-listed **Hala Ludowa** is a truly remarkable building. Built in Gotham City style in 1913, the architect Max Berg was way ahead of his time: his use of reinforced concrete, and the huge unsupported dome of the 6,000-seater auditorium in particular feels like a much later structure. To see inside you may have to buy a ticket for a performance, preferably Wagner, whose pieces suit the scale and style of the building perfectly.

Top tip In high season buy tickets to the Racławice Panorama early as the numbers allowed inside are limited and it's incredibly popular with Polish tour groups.

---

some simply superb vistas then head off to explore the nearby **Church of SS Peter and Paul**, the **Church of the Holy Cross** and the **Church of St Mary on the Sands**, all remarkable buildings in their own right.

TAKING A BREAK

Wrocław explorers are naturally drawn to the Rynek for a refreshment break. In summer, the city's premier piazza sprouts sunshades under which visitors can enjoy slightly overpriced fare from the local cafés. Otherwise, Wrocław's huge student population ensures it is well stocked with a choice of cheap and cheerful cafés.

➕ 194 B4

Tourist Information Centre
✉ Rynek 14 ☎ 071 344 3111; www.wroclaw.pl ⏰ Summer 9–9, winter 9–8

Town Hall
✉ Rynek ☎ 071 347 1693; www.mmw.pl ⏰ Wed–Sat 11–5, Sun 10–6
💷 Moderate

Racławice Panorama
✉ ul. Purkyniego 11 ☎ 071 344 2344; www.panoramaraclawicka.pl
⏰ Summer daily 9–5; winter Tue–Sun 9–4 💷 Expensive

View over the River Odra and the red roofs of Wrocław

2 Zamek Książ

This tour-bus favourite is a monster of a building perched on a promontory of bedrock high above the River Pełcznica. The castle is one of the most popular visitor hotspots in Silesia despite only a few of the rooms being open to the public.

Behind the enormous pink façade are more than 400 rooms

Książ started life as a 13th-century fortress belonging to Duke Bolko I and, added to over the centuries, was eventually acquired by the wealthy Prussian Hochberg family in the 17th century, who converted it into a luxurious palace. The Nazis used the castle as a headquarters and after the war the Red Army moved in. All occupants have left their mark here and the castle displays a hotchpotch of styles, from original Romanesque elements to 20th-century additions. From a distance Książ looks rather like three separate castles all trying to push each other from the foothold of rock they occupy.

Visitors have the option of taking a guided tour or exploring on their own, following the signposting as they go. Of the rooms open to the public, the best are the ornate baroque **Maximilian Hall** and the rococo Green Room. However, some feel the real highlight of the tour is the ascent of the castle **tower**, which affords magnificent views of the surrounding forested hills, best seen in autumn when they burst into a riot of colour.

TAKING A BREAK

There are refreshment stops on the approaches to the castle and below the ramparts overlooking the river.

➕ 194 A3 ✉ ul. Piastów Śląskich 1 ☎ 074 664 3834; www.ksiaz.walbrzych.pl 🕐 Summer Mon–Fri 10–5, Sat, Sun 10–6, closed Mon in winter 💷 Moderate

3 Świdnica & Jawor Peace Churches

Poland has countless timber churches but none are of such significance as the peace churches of Silesia. Listed by UNESCO as World Heritage Sites in 2001, the "peace" refers to the state of affairs finalised by the Treaty of Westphalia in 1648 which formally ended the Thirty Years' War.

Under the terms of the agreement the staunchly Catholic Habsburgs had to allow the construction of three Protestant churches on their territory as an act of tolerance. These were situated in Świdnica south of Wrocław, Jawor 50km (31 miles) to the west and Głogów to the northeast (the latter burned down in 1758) and were built according to strict Habsburg stipulations (no nails, stone or bells and all work to be completed within one year). These rules were disregarded as soon as the Prussians took over in Silesia in the late 18th century, hence the stonework you may see.

Świdnica's peace church is the more popular of the two, perhaps as the town is a worthwhile destination in its

Jawor peace church was listed as a World Heritage Site in 2001

The beautiful baroque interior of Jawor peace church

own right. The large monochrome half-timbered structure (250m/272 yards southeast of the Rynek), dating from 1652, holds an incredibly ornate and atmospheric baroque interior, unusual for normally austere Protestant places of worship. The pews are packed tightly together to squeeze in as big a congregation as possible (up to 4,000). Similar Jawor (1654) is slightly larger, not quite as ornate and receives fewer visitors than it deserves. Both are still used for religious purposes as well as concerts and recitals.

TAKING A BREAK

The main square in each town is the best place to head for nourishment.

Świdnica Peace Church
➕ 194 A3 ✉ Plac Pokoju 6 ☎ 074 852 2814; www.kosciolpokoju.pl 🕐 Apr–Oct Mon–Sat 9–5, Sun 3–5, reservations required in winter ✋ Inexpensive

Jawor Peace Church
➕ 194 A4 ✉ Park Pokoju 1 ☎ 076 870 5145 🕐 Apr–Oct Mon–Sat 10–5, Sun 12–5, reservations required in winter ✋ Inexpensive

ŚWIDNICA & JAWOR PEACE CHURCHES: INSIDE INFO

Top tip It is possible to **visit both churches** on a day trip from Wrocław. If you don't have your own vehicle, buses and trains link the two towns.

At Your Leisure

❹ Nysa

If the bombs of World War II hadn't destroyed 80 per cent of this small Silesian town 75km (46 miles) south of Wrocław, Nysa would be one of Poland's most attractive centres. Fortunately this once important religious centre rebuilt its impressive dark redbrick Cathedral of St James, which originally dated from 1420. The steeply sloping roof covers an austere lofty Gothic interior, the sombre picture broken only by numerous side-chapels. Back outside, the hulk of a freestanding belfry that was never finished, now stands derelict with its war damage on show.

Cathedral of St James and St Agnes, Nysa

The local museum (ul. Jarosławka 11) displays a scale model of the town at its peak as well as exhibits documenting the damage done during the war. The only other sight of note is the Church of SS Peter and Paul, containing some exquisite Baroque frill.

➕ 194 B3
Tourist Information Office
✉ ul. Bracka 4 ☎ 077 433 4171

❺ Paczków

During the 19th century, most towns and cities in central and Eastern Europe tore down their town walls, which were becoming unsightly and stifling economic growth. For some reason, the enlightened citizens of Paczków, halfway between Kłodzko

and Nysa, never deemed this necessary and bequeathed posterity an entire set of medieval fortifications complete with three barbicans (called the Wrocław, Ząbkow and Kłodzko gates) and 19 of the original 24 watchtowers. These encircle the Rynek and a few streets that haven't survived the centuries so historically intact. However, the Church of St John, a Gothic and Renaissance fortified cube, strikes an impressive pose just beyond the main square.

➕ 194 B2

❻ Międzygórze

The name of this tranquil oasis in the far south of the Kłodzko region – a chunk of Polish territory surrounded on three sides by the Czech Republic – means literally "amid the mountains" and it is hiking into the surrounding wooded uplands that draws visitors to this far-flung corner. The village itself boasts some Tyrolean-style timber chalets and is an excellent base from where to summit Śnieżnik, the highest peak in the region (1426m/4,677ft), which is shared with the Czechs (who call it Králický Sněžník). At the top there is a mountain refuge, actually a fairly comfortable guesthouse called Schronisko na śnieżniku operated by the Polish Tourist Association (PTTK). Marked walking trails head out from Międzygórze to the top of Śnieżnik and to many other local places of natural beauty.

➕ 194 A2
Tourist Information Office
✉ ul. Wojska Polskiego 2 ☎ 074 813 5195

❼ Kłodzko

This engaging regional centre is a natural base for discovering the Ziemia Kłodzka, a triangular piece of Poland which resembles an arrowhead puncturing the Czech Republic to the south. Your exploration of the old town nestled

Kłodzko Fortress looks out over the town

at an angle below a low-rise fortress should begin at the Franciscan Church, a double-spired baroque affair which guards the approach to the town's pride and joy, an intact Gothic Bridge lined with baroque statuary – a kind of mini version of Prague's Charles Bridge. Its short span takes you across the Mlynówka Stream (a tributary of the Nysa Kłodzka River, which flows a few hundred metres to the east) and onto the Rynek. This is a sloping cobbled expanse with a large 19th-century town hall at its centre containing two good restaurants.

Exit the square uphill to the northwest and climb to the huge Kłodzka Fortress, the largest in Poland measuring 17ha (42 acres). Its stone walls house various exhibitions

including several veteran fire engines and a section on local glass.

Admire the views across the town and surrounding countryside before retracing your steps down the hill to access the Underground Tourist Route, a complex of medieval cellars that descends from the foot of the fortress to the parish church. This soot-stained Gothic edifice is long overdue a good sandblasting and although an impressive place of worship, it is normally closed to visitors except during services.

🚗 194 A2
Tourist Information Office
✉ Plac Bolesława Chrobrego 1
☎ 074 865 8970

8 Kudowa-Zdrój

Most Poles heading to Kudowa-Zdrój will be doing so to ease ailments at the local spa, the largest in the Ziemia Kłodzka. The large spa park and pump room where you can sample the local mineral water are relaxing areas, but most foreigners come here to visit the ghoulish Chapel of Skulls 1km (0.5 mile) to the north, in the grounds of the Church of St Bartholomew in the adjacent village of Czermna. The walls of the chapel are decorated with the skulls of at least 3,000 victims of the Thirty

A typical example of timber architecture in the mountain village of Międzygórze

The baroque-style Church of Assumption

Years War and various conflicts and plagues to hit the region between the 15th and the 18th century. The chapel was the macabre idea of a Czech, Václav Tomášek, Czermna parish priest in the late 18th century. After he spent eight years filling the chapel with the contents of mass graves across the region, his own skull joined the others when he died. This is the only place of its kind in Poland but the Czechs, obviously taken with this controversial trend in church décor, boast a slightly better known bone-filled chapel in Kutná Hora.
🕂 194 A2
Chapel of Skulls
✉ ul. Moniuszki 8 ☎ 074 866 1754
🕐 Tue Sun 9.30–5.30, shorter hours in winter

🟦 Krzeszów

This tiny village in the hills to the southwest of Wałbrzych has not one but two remarkable churches, some of the finest examples of central European baroque in Poland. The Church of St Joseph, the older and smaller of the two, dates from the 1690s and although the facade is relatively unexciting, the interior more than makes up for it, with frescoes by Michael Willman depicting the life of Joseph and much rich baroque and swirling rococo decoration.

The larger Church of the Assumption was raised in the early 18th century and is a true baroque masterpiece with paintings by Bohemian artist Petr Brandl and frescoes by Willman's grandson, Neunhertz. Behind the altar is a mausoleum containing the remains

of 14th-century Silesian duke, Prince Bolko I, and others of his line. The two churches are part of an abbey complex in the middle of the village.
🕂 188 C1

🔟 Jelenia Góra

This quiet town of 100,000 souls in the far west of Silesia is a fairly interesting place in itself but is normally a jumping-off point for the beautiful Karkonosze National

The quiet town square of Jelenia Góra

Park to the south. The town, which celebrated its 900th anniversary in 2008, has a traffic-free historical centre, which emerged almost unscathed from World War II and boasts a number of churches. The focal point is the Plac Ratuszowy (Town Hall Square) lined with photogenic arcaded burghers' town houses that look upon the 18th-century town hall. Some 500m (545 yards) south of the square you will find the Karkonosze Regional Museum (ul. Matejki 28) where the traditional glass-making tradition of the Karkonosze area is the principal focus. The Karkonosze Mountains lie to the south and straddle the Czech border, 16km (10 miles) away.
🕂 188 C1
Tourist Information Office
✉ Bankowa 27 ☎ 075 767 6925;
www.jelenia.gora.pl

Where to... Stay

Prices

Expect to pay per night for a double room (in peak season):
€ under 200PLN   €€ 200PLN–500PLN   €€€ over 500PLN

KŁODZKO

Hotel Korona €

You will have stayed in more charming places than this nondescript motel on the outskirts of Kłodzko, but it's a reasonable place to stay in town. Inside it's basic but comfortable and there's a sound restaurant.

➕ 194 A2 ☒ ul. Noworudzka 1 ☎ 074 867 3737; www.hotel-korona.pl

ZAMEK KSIĄŻ

Hotel Zamkowy €€

Few visitors stay over in Książ, most preferring to return to the comfort of Wrocław and its big-city delights. If you do choose to stay the night, this new hotel housed in a section of the castle complex is the best option. Rooms are little on the sparse side but generously cut, and with the castle tours only a short hop away the location is perfect. Breakfast is an extra 15PLN per person.

➕ 194 A3 ☒ ul. Piastów Śląskich 1 ☎ 074 665 4144; www.hotelzamkowy.pl

WROCŁAW

Dwór Polski €€

Situated between the Rynek and ul. Kiełbaśnicza, there's no more central place to get a good night's sleep in all Wrocław. As far as your room is concerned, it's a lottery as to whether you are assigned a 16th-century chamber or naff 1980s period piece, so ask to see what you are getting before you commit. The building also houses a range of eateries including a medieval Polish tavern, a fancy Lithuanian coffee house and rural-style *karczma*. There is a 20 per cent discount on accommodation at weekends.

➕ 194 B4 ☒ ul. Kiełbaśnicza 2 ☎ 071 372 3415; www.dworpolski.wroclaw.pl

Hotel Jana Pawła II €€

This brand-new four-star place can be found on the corner of a quiet street near the cathedral. A well-composed blend of new glass and old tenement from the outside, the theme continues inside with shiny new communal spaces and guest accommodation that is up-to-the-minute and tastefully furnished. Some rooms benefit from picturesque views of the Ostrów Tumski, possibly the reason both incumbent president Lech Kaczyński and former head of state, Lech Wałęsa, chose to stay here on visits to the city. There are also facilities for visitors with a disability.

➕ 194 B4 ☒ ul. św Idziego 2 ☎ 071 327 1400; www.pensjonat-jp2.pl

ŚWIDNICA

Park Hotel €€

It's not easy to overlook the mock fortress around 1km (0.5 miles) south of the Rynek which houses this sound if not-too-imaginative three-star place entered via a ballustraded stairway. Rooms are spotless and comfortable enough but seem to come either overfurnished or spartan. Ask to see your accommodation before you commit so you can choose which you prefer. Staying here means you have easy access to one of Świdnica's better restaurants.

➕ 194 A3 ☒ ul. Pionierów 20 ☎ 074 853 7722; www.park-hotel.com.pl/

Where to...
Eat and Drink

Prices

Expect to pay for a three-course meal for one, excluding drinks:
€ under 50PLN   €€ 50PLN–100PLN   €€€ over 100PLN

Cztery Pory Roku €€

The "Four Seasons" located on Jelenia Góra's main piazza is a relative newcomer to the town's dining scene but competes well with other more established eateries. The dining space is decorated in warm colours, the service is polite and the atmosphere relaxed. The menu features reasonably priced hearty Polish dishes including roast pork in garlic, duck breast with apple

and cranberry, sirloin in forest mushrooms, wild boar forest goulash and cheesecake.
🚹 188 C1 ⊠ Plac Ratuszowy 39
☎ 075 752 2140 ⓕ Daily 10am–11pm

Restauracja Książęca €€

The restaurant attached to the Hotel Zamkowy is arguably the best place to eat around the castle. Feast on platters of well-prepared meat and fish under the arched vaulting of the spacious banqueting hall.

The menu is a blend of Polish and international and vegetarians are also catered too.
🚹 194 A3 ⊠ ul. Piastów Śląskich 1
☎ 074 840 5862 ⓕ Daily 10am–11pm

Bar Pizzeria Romano €

Housed under lofty Gothic-style vaulting, the town hall's "other" restaurant is an aesthetically more impressive affair, though the ambience is disturbed by the radio. The pizza menu features all the usual suspects, which require no translation. Admittedly, this comes as a bit of relief from heavy Polish meat dishes, though for a far more local experience go to the other side of the town hall to W Ratuszu.
🚹 194 A2 ⊠ Plac B. Chrobrego
☎ 074 867 0935 ⓕ Daily 10–10

W Ratuszu €

The name of this central place literally means "in the town hall" and that's exactly where you'll

find it. Enter from the western side of the building to be greeted by a large stained-glass Czech lion rampant, the town's coat of arms reflecting the time it spent under Bohemian rule. Inside you'll discover Kłodzko's most respected eatery, with wood panelling, polite service, a relatively formal ambience and an unchallenging menu of international and central European standards. In summer the outdoor tables are a great place to cradle a beer and watch the world climb by.
🚹 194 A2 ⊠ Plac B. Chrobrego
☎ 074 865 8145 ⓕ Daily 10–10

JaDka €€€

With its excellent service and finely crafted dishes, this is top-notch dining in the heart of Wrocław's historical centre. The menu is an eclectic mix of European influences from Spanish and Italian to Lithuanian and Russian. All this is enjoyed in an understated interior

beneath impressive vaulted brick ceilings. Although dining here is on the expensive side, the three-course lunch menu is an affordable 35PLN.
🖂 ul Rzeźnicza 24/25 ☎ 071 343 6461
🕒 Daily noon–11pm

Piwnica Świdnicka €€

You know you've come to the right place when a plaque at the entrance to a central European restaurant lists Goethe and Chopin as previous guests. This 600-year-old tavern occupies a veritable warren of themed cellars beneath the town hall and is so big you may have to download a map from the internet before you go! The well turned-out waiters serve up fiendishly large portions of pork knuckle, wild boar steaks, Wiener schnitzel and other heavyweight fare, which you can sluice down with a stein or two of ale. This is a superior alternative to the popular but touristy Spiz microbrewery in the same building.
🚏 194 B4 🖂 Rynek-Ratusz 1 ☎ 071 369 9510 🕒 Daily noon–midnight

Pod Złotym Jeleniem €€

Easily identified by the large golden stag (hence the name Under the Golden Stag) above the door of an ochre town house in the northeastern corner of the Rynek, this eatery invites guests to munch on slabs of wild boar, wild duck, roe deer and fish, all bagged by local hunters and brought to your table straight off the grill. Slightly on the pricier side but with portion sizes this big, you won't need to eat for the rest of the day. The downstairs cellar is better than the upstairs dining room and this place is at its most enjoyable when check-full and raucous.
🚏 194 B4 🖂 Rynek 44 ☎ 071 372 3951
🕒 Daily noon–1am

Pod Gryfami

Housed in an impressively gabled town house on the Rynek, this fascinating café/bar/restaurant has a wide selection of spaces, from intimate cellars to first-floor formal. Period junk lines the walls and the prettily laid restaurant tables are encircled by plush wing-back chairs. Most diners are too busy looking at the décor to order very quickly, but when the waiter does appear you can choose from expertly prepared Polish and international meat and fish dishes or simply opt for a coffee and ice cream. This was voted one of the top ten restaurants in Wrocław in 2008.
🚏 194 B4 🖂 Rynek 2 ☎ 071 344 3389
🕒 Daily 2–11

St Petersburg €€€

If you thought Russian cuisine was all about overboiled cabbage and vodka, the St Petersburg, just a few steps off the main square, will come as a pleasant surprise. Delicious and unexpectedly imaginative dishes such as aubergine stuffed with chicken in dill sauce and wild rice or veal stewed in wine with grilled aubergine are served by extremely helpful waiters in an opulent wood panelled dining room. This is definitely a place to come to mark a special occasion and reservations are advised.
🚏 194 B4 🖂 ul. Igielna ☎ 071 341 8084
🕒 Daily noon–midnight

ŚWIDNICA

Kurna Chata €

The winning combination of low prices, simple Polish meat dishes, a convenient central location and friendly service make this branch of a Silesian chain the best dining option in Świdnica. The menu is printed onto cloth and the decor is an attempt at re-creating the homey interior of a Polish country cottage. The dishes are filling and tasty and there are several vegetarian mains available such as baked broccoli, fried cheese and mushroom-filled *pierogi*. Make sure you get there early around mealtimes as this place is understandably popular.
🚏 194 A3 🖂 Rynek 35 ☎ 074 851 3488
🕒 Daily 10am–11pm

Where to...
Shop

Wrocław is Silesia's shopping centre and, apart from a few souvenirs at Ksiaz Castle and glass from the Karkonosze Mountains, your złoty are most likely to be frittered away here.

MALLS AND MARKETS

Wrocław's **covered market**, occupying a disused 19th-century railway station on the banks of the Odra, is a colourful and fragrant experience but is invariably overlooked by visitors to the city. Wrocław also has a large city-centre shopping mall, the **Galeria Dominikanska** (www.galeria-dominikanska.pl) packed to the roof with brand name outlets such as Mango, Benetton, C&A, Nike and New Yorker. The centre also has 12 eateries where you can drop from your shop.

GLASS

The Karkonosze Mountains and Ziemia Kłodzka have a long tradition of glass-making and handcrafted items make beautiful reminders of your trip. Look out for local artists' galleries or ask at information centres where the best places to buy can be found.

WALKING MAPS

One of the most popular activities in Silesia is hitting the mesh of marked hiking trails in the Karkonosze Mountains. The best maps to guide you on your way are the Polish Karkonosze maps published by EKO-GRAF or the Czech VKÚ-KČT map series, sheet 22 (Krkonoše), which covers both sides of the border.

Where to...
Be Entertained

Wrocław is the unchallenged cultural hub of the entire region, with a particular focus on high-brow music and opera, and, with a huge student population, it also has a lively nightlife scene.

MUSIC

Classical music is big news in Wrocław, with an opera company (www.opera.wroclaw.pl), a philharmonic orchestra (www.filharmonia.wroclaw.pl) and a huge musical academy (www.amuz.wroc.pl). One of the most impressive venues is the Hala Ludowa (www.halaludowawroc.pl), where classical and pop music concerts are occasionally held in between trade fairs, exhibitions and sports events.

SPORT

Wrocław has been selected to host some matches for the 2012 European Football Championships – which will no doubt bring an influx of visitors to the city.

WHAT'S ON

The excellent listings guide *In Your Pocket* is given out gratis at the tourist information centre. The **Lower Silesia Cultural Information Centre** (www.okis.pl) stocks information on what's on in Wrocław and around, as well as selling tickets for many events. Contact the tourist offices in other towns to find out what's happening on the culture front in their area.

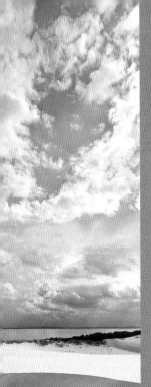

The Northwest

Getting Your Bearings

The northwest of Poland is made up of the regions of Pomerania and Wielkopolska, both of which have spent considerable periods within the borders of Germany. Poles associate Pomerania with beach fun and the Baltic where many city dwellers still decamp in the hotter months of the year. Inland Wielkopolska is Poland's historical heartland, where the first Polish state rose in the 10th century, and thus has great significance for Polish national identity.

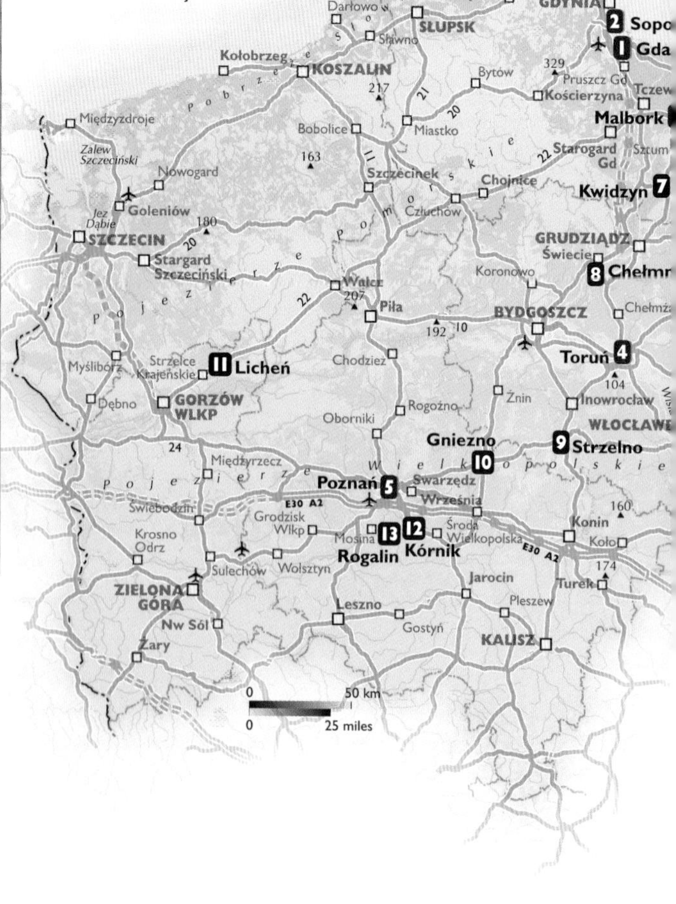

Władysławowo

Ustka   Wejherowo   Hel **6**

Darłowo   Lębork   **GDYNIA**   **2** Sopo

Słowno   **SŁUPSK**   **1** Gda

Kołobrzeg   Bytów   329   Pruszcz Gd

KOSZALIN   217   Kościerzyna   Tczew

Międzyzdroje   Bobolice   Miastko   **Malbork**

Zalew   Starogard   Sztum

Szczeciński   163   Szczecinek   Gd

Nowogard   Chojnice   **Kwidzyn** **7**

Jez   Goleniów   180   Człuchów

Dąbie   **GRUDZIĄDZ**

SZCZECIN   Świecie   **8** Chełmr

Stargard   Koronowo

Szczeciński   Wałcz   207   Chełmża

Piła   **BYDGOSZCZ**

192   10

Myślibórz   Strzelce   **11** Licheń   Chodzież   **Toruń** **4**

Krajeńskie   104

Dębno   **GORZÓW**   Rogoźno   Inowrocław

WLKP   Oborniki   Żnin   **WŁOCŁAWE**

24   **Gniezno**   **9** Strzelno

Międzyrzecz   **Wielko** p o l s k i e   **10**

Świebodzin   **Poznań** **5**   Swarzędz

E30 A2   Września   160

Krosno   Grodzisk   Środa   Konin

Odrz   Wlkp   Mosina   Wielkopolska E30 A2   Koło

Sulechów   Wolsztyn   **Rogalin**   **13** **12**   174

Kórnik   Jarocin   Turek

ZIELONA   Leszno   Pleszew

GÓRA   Gostyń

Nw Sól   **KALISZ**

Żary

0   50 km

0   25 miles

Getting Your Bearings   139

Right: Visitors can examine the intricate palm leaf vaulting in the Winter Refectory at Malbork Castle

Page 137: Gorda Lacka Dunes, Gdańsk

★ Don't Miss

Above: St Vojtěch's silver shrine, Gniezno
Below: View from the lighthouse at Sopot

The Poland story, to all intents and purposes, began in the city of Poznań on the Ostrów Tumski (Tumski Island) in the 10th century under Piast Duke Mieszko I, Poland's earliest recorded ruler and the first to be baptised. However, the capital of the fledgling state was established in Kraków, with Poznań and Gniezno remaining important regional centres of power. Due to its position on the coast, Pomerania was always important for trade, a fact not lost on the Teutonic Knights who overran the region in the 14th century. Both provinces were seized by Prussia in the Partitions of the 18th century, and even after the Treaty of Versailles reinstated Poland as a state in 1919, this area remained, for the most part, German soil until Poland's borders were redrawn following World War II.

No visit to Pomerania would be complete without at least a day in Gdańsk, the region's trump card. Sandy beaches and dunes extend along the Baltic coast to the German border and inland are some beautifully preserved historical town centres such as Toruń and Gniezno as well as Gothic Malbork, Poland's top castle. The epicentre of Wielkopolska is Poznań, Poland's trade fair capital and a vibrant, forward-looking city of 600,000 inhabitants.

In Four Days

If you're not quite sure where to begin your travels, this itinerary recommends a practical and enjoyable four days in the Northwest, taking in some of the best places to see using the Getting Your Bearings map on the previous page. For more information see the main entries.

Day One

Morning
Start the day over a coffee in a terrace café in **①Gdańsk's** (➤ 142–144) pretty Mariacka Street (above), before striking out to explore the beautifully restored Main Town. Lunch in style at Kresowa or Gdańska (➤ 157).

Afternoon and Evening
Hop across the river to visit the Maritime Museum before taking in the sights of the Old Town, including the shipyard and the Roads to Freedom Exhibition for some recent historical background. In the late afternoon you could just make it to **②Sopot** (➤ 145) to catch some last rays on the beach or for a promenade along the pier before hitting a beachside club or relaxing with a cocktail at the Grand Hotel.

Day Two

Morning
Today it's south all the way, starting at **3** **Malbork** castle (left, ➤ 146–147). Emerge from the long tour just in time for lunch at the Piwniczka tavern (➤ 157).

Afternoon and Evening
Toruń is today's final destination but as you journey south, make a couple of stops at the historical towns of **7** **Kwidzyn** and **8** **Chełmno** along the way (➤ 152).

Day Three

Morning
Historical **4** **Toruń** (➤ 148–149) can be seen in a long morning, though you may want to linger for a while at the Copernicus Museum. Lunch at one of the town's lively eateries, then continue on south.

Afternoon and Evening
Your journey to Poznań will take you via **9** **Strzelno** (➤ 153) and **10** **Gniezno** (➤ 153) where more Gothic bricks await in their millions. A late evening arrival in Poznań is just about the right time to join the crowds of drinkers and diners at the vibrant Brovaria on the central square.

Day Four

Morning
Discover **5** **Poznań's** (➤ 150–151) pretty rebuilt centre (right) at your leisure, making sure you visit the town hall and cathedral on your way and perhaps stopping late morning for a light lunch at the Stary Browar shopping mall.

Afternoon and Evening
Leave the busy city and head south to the double act of noble residences at **12** **Kórnik** (➤ 154) and **13** **Rogalin** (➤ 155) just a short distance apart.

0 Gdańsk

Amber, shipyards, Lech Wałęsa and the golden years of Baltic trade – Gdańsk on the north coast is famous for many things and is by far the northwest's top attraction. The bombs of World War II left this proud city in ruins, but now budget flights from Western Europe flood the painstakingly restored historical centre with tourists. Gdańsk is also an ideal base for exploring the Tri-City area of Gdańsk, Sopot and Gdynia.

Główne Miasto and Waterfront

The city's principal attractions are in the Główne Miasto or Main Town, a network of old streets between the river, the railway station and ul. Podwale Staromiejskie. **Ul. Długa** and

GDAŃSK: INSIDE INFO

In more depth The humble lighthouse at the mouth of the river has had a fascinating history. Until 1939 it lived a peaceful life as lighthouse, harbour pilot's tower and timeball station. However, on September 1 1939, the day Hitler invaded Poland, the Polish garrison at the Westerplatte on the opposite side of the river took fire from German troops positioned at the top of the lighthouse, which was partially destroyed in the ensuing battle. These were the very first shots fired in World War II. Today the new owner has renovated the lighthouse to its pre-war state and now runs it as a private museum.

Survey the town from St Mary's church bell tower

Długi Targ together form the route of the Royal Way, leading from the Upland Gate in the west to the Green Gate by the river. On the way, café-, restaurant- and shop-lined ul. Długa, the city's showpiece thoroughfare, passes some of the best-known sights, such as the Amber Museum, the **Neptune Fountain**, the **town hall** housing the **Gdańsk History Museum** and the **Artus Court**, a former meeting place for Gdańsk's merchants, containing some finely restored chambers.

Passing through the Green Gate, a former royal residence, you find yourself on the **waterfront**, where once ships unloaded their cargoes but now cafés and restaurants serve the tourists. The foremost attraction along its length is the dark timber **Gdańsk Crane**, the largest lifting device in medieval Europe when it was built in the mid-15th century. The crane now belongs to the **Maritime Museum**, whose main building lies across the water.

Several gates along the quayside provide access back into the Główne Miasto, but the one you should choose is the Mariacka Gate leading to **ul. Mariacka**. Often lauded as the most picturesque street in Poland, this moody lane is truly unique, with its wrought-iron hand rails twisting down to the cobbles, gargoyles spitting rainwater at passers-by, and quirky pieces of sculpture and terraces outside each house, several of which host outdoor seating for cafés. Billed as the largest brick-built church in the world, the Gothic hulk of **St Mary's Church** almost blocks the far end of the street. It is estimated that the nave can hold up to 25,000 people, and 31 chapels and 300 tombstones grace the interior.

Stare Miasto

The Stare Miasto or Old Town extends north of ul. Podwale Staromiejskie to the famous shipyard. In front of the gates you will find the powerful Monument to Fallen Shipyard Workers, commemorating those killed during the strikes of 1970.

Other places of interest in the Old Town include the Great Mill (now a shopping centre), several large red-brick churches, including St Bridget's, with its amazing amber altar, and the Old Town Hall, which miraculously escaped World War II intact and now serves as a cultural centre and concert venue.

Other Attractions

Situated in the desirable suburb of Oliwa to the northwest of the city centre, attractive **Oliwa Cathedral** is a real mix of styles with its baroque entrance, red-brick octagonal Renaissance towers and lofty Gothic nave, the longest in Poland. The cathedral's showpiece is the rococo organ, which contains almost 8,000 pipes and is used for free organ concerts. Around the cathedral extends Oliwa Park, where you will also find the **Bishop's Palace** and a small **ethnographical museum** with exhibits from the fascinating ethnically distinct Kashuba region to the south. To get to Oliwa, take the SKM train to Gdańsk Oliwa station.

Gdańsk Crane on the waterfront is a medieval marvel

TAKING A BREAK

Watch the world file past and the amber sellers at work over a coffee or lunch on the terrace of the **Café Mariacka** (ul. Mariacka 21), one of the best-loved cafés in the city.

✚ 184 C4

Tourist Information Centre
✉ ul. Długa 45 ☎ 058 301 9151 🕐 Mon–Fri 9–6, Sat, Sun 8:30–4:30

Gdańsk History Museum
✉ ul. Długa 47 ☎ 058 767 9100; www.mhmg.gda.pl 🕐 Summer Mon 11–3, Tue–Sat 10–6 Sun 11–6; shorter hours in winter 🎫 Moderate

Maritime Museum
✉ ul. Ołowianka 9–13 ☎ 058 301 8611; www.cmm.pl 🕐 Summer Tue–Sun 10–6; shorter hours in winter 🎫 Moderate

❷ Sopot

A short drive or commuter train trip from Gdańsk, the most fun-loving settlement in the Tri-City is laid-back Sopot where it's buckets and spades on the beach and strolls along the pier by day, funky nightlife and beach parties by night, all set against a Baltic backdrop.

This summer-time haunt of Poland's rich and famous could be a world away from the shipyards and grand merchant past of Gdańsk. Heading down from the railway station, the main pedestrianised café- and boutique-lined ul. Bohaterów Monte Cassino is busy night and day with holidaymakers strolling to or from the beach, ice creams in hand. Half-way along you cannot fail to notice the Crooked House (Krzywy Dom), a wackily incongruous piece of post-Communist architecture containing shops and restaurants.

If you thought Poland's timber churches were an odd idea, wait until you discover Europe's longest wooden pier consisting of 500m (545 yards) of timber stilts rammed into the sand, atop which runs a boardwalk. The original temporary structure was dismantled every autumn and stored away to protect it from the Baltic storms but a permanent pier was erected in the early 20th century. Needless to say, the waves have swept it away several times, most recently in 2004. In peak holiday season there's a small admission fee to walk its length. Either side of the pier extend wide sandy beaches lapped by the (usually very cold) Baltic Sea.

Sopot's wooden pier has charmed visitors for more than a hundred years

TAKING A BREAK

Take a break from the holiday crowds at the quaint **Kawiarnia u Hrabiego** at ul. Czyżewskiego 12, a 19th-century cafe hideaway with creaky floorboards, net curtains and heaps of old-fashioned spa-town charisma.

➕ 184 C4

Tourist Information Office
✉ ul. Dworcowa 4 ☎ 058 550 3783; www.sopot.pl

SOPOT: INSIDE INFO

Top tip If you are in the party mood, the **dunes** to the west of Sopot are home to a string of bars and nightclubs, regarded as Poland's most vibrant nightlife strip. In the summer months Varsovians and other inland city dwellers flock here for all-night beach fun.

3 Malbork

History has bequeathed Poland scores of castles and chateaux in a whole host of shapes and styles but none can compare to the mountain of red brick that is Malbork. The sheer extent of the building, its riverside location, proximity to Gdańsk and extra large-size history makes this Teutonic Gothic pile one of Poland's most visited attractions and a must-see for anyone holidaying in the region.

Some History

Malbork first hit the history books in the late 13th century when the Teutonic knights established their headquarters here, from which they ruled all of northern Poland. Over the next two centuries the castle increased in size and stature but was then sold off by the cash-strapped knights to the Czechs, who passed it on to the Polish king for a hefty mark-up. Polish royals used Malbork as a residence for three centuries until the fortress fell to Prussia in the partitions of the late 18th century, after which it served as a barracks. Used as a POW camp during World War II, it was left in ruins by a Red Army

The imposing red castle seen from the opposite bank of the River Nogat attack in 1945. Meticulous renovation work, which has been ongoing ever since, led to the castle's listing by UNESCO as a World Heritage Site in 1997.

The Castle

Everything you see within the fortress is part of the **Malbork Castle Museum** created in 1961. Whichever way you decide to enter the castle (English/Polish tour, private guide), your first port of call after crossing the first drawbridge is the courtyard of the **Middle Castle**, dating back to the early days of the Teutonic Knights. To your right rises the **Grand Master's Palace**, to the left lie some renovated exhibition spaces where a dazzling display of amber and a working mock-up of a castle kitchen assault the senses. Another drawbridge brings you to the High Castle, the oldest part of the fortress, where you'll find some exquisite Gothic spaces such as the treasury, the Chapter House and noble accommodation for various Teutonic VIPs. Your next stop should be the **Church of Our Lady**, once a magnificent place of worship all but obliterated by the Soviet assault in 1945. Renovation work here is set to last for many years and visiting the church gives an idea of the devastation which was wrought on Malbork. A long corridor leads from the church to the Castle's **central tower**, which can be climbed for an extra fee. These are just the highlights of a huge castle and guided tours visit many more rooms, halls, chambers and corridors. You also shouldn't miss the best **view of the castle** from the opposite bank of the River Nogat, which can be reached via a wooden footbridge. This is the only location from which huge Malbork can be photographed in its entirety.

TAKING A BREAK

In summer Malbork is filled by an army of fast-food stands, serving up sausages, chips, burgers and the like. For a sit-down meal, try **Piwniczka** (➤ 157) within the castle walls or the tour-bus restaurant at the Hotel Zamek.

🕂 184 C3 ✉ ul. Starościńska 1 ☎ 055 647 0976; www.zamek.malbork.pl
🕔 Summer 9–7; shorter hours in winter 🎫 Expensive

MALBORK CASTLE: INSIDE INFO

Top tip The standard **guided tours** of Malbork Castle are notoriously long (around three hours) but there are ways of seeing the Gothic interiors in less time. Firstly, it is possible to buy a detailed guide, join a Polish language tour and then quietly slip away to explore on your own (though getting lost is a risk). Better still, hire your own guide through the tourist office back in Gdańsk and put a time limit on your visit.

In more detail Notice the **small plaques** around the castle featuring devils in various positions. These are Gothic signposts to the many toilets there once were in the castle. Crossed legs and extended wings meant it was still a long way to the nearest loo and the devil's beard indicated the direction to head.

4 Toruń

The birthplace of one of Poland's most celebrated sons, Nicolaus Copernicus, is one of the few bona fide medieval cities to have emerged unscathed from World War II. With its spruced up red-brick churches, cobbled medieval lanes, grand central square and intact riverside fortifications, this UNESCO-listed cultural hotspot is a must-see attraction.

Copernicus's City

A tour of Toruń's historical nucleus traditionally begins on the Rynek Staromiejski (Old Town Square), dominated by the **town hall**. Originally built in the 14th century, this brick mountain now accommodates a museum. The 40m (131-foot) tower is ascendable and affords sweeping views. On the western flank of the Rynek stand two old churches, St Mary's to the northwest and the Church of the Holy Ghost in the southwest corner. At the southeast corner of the hall stands one of Toruń's most photographed sights, a bronze **statue of Copernicus** holding one of his heliocentric models.

Continuing with the Copernicus theme, one block south of the Rynek is the attractive Gothic merchant's house where the astronomer was born in 1473. This is now a **museum** dedicated to his life and work and includes a full-scale model of medieval Toruń, the focus of a light and sound show. At the eastern end of ul. Kopernika be sure not to miss the **Cathedral of St John the Baptist**, Toruń's oldest place of worship, begun in 1260. The highlights here are the bell (the second largest in Poland) that hangs in the 52m (170-foot) tower and the font where Copernicus was baptised.

Statue of the revolutionary astronomer Nicolaus Copernicus

Riverfront and New Town

From the cathedral there are several routes through the rest of the Old Town. Head south and you will hit the Vistula, which, by the time it reaches Toruń, has swollen into a broad and mighty river. The entire 600m (654-yard) flank along the riverbank is lined with defensive walls and watchtowers which once encircled the town and which provide a pleasant backdrop to a riverside stroll. Alternatively, walk north to ul. Szeroka, the main pedestrian thoroughfare lined with shops and cafés. This will eventually bring you to the New

Town Square, which is considerably less spectacular than its older neighbour. However, in the eastern corner the scene is livened up a little by the Gothic **Church of St James** with its exterior flying buttresses and interior of gaudy baroque. Your last stop should be the **Church of St Catherine** on busy ul. Warszawska, one of the finest examples anywhere in Poland of the 19th-century revival in Gothic redbrick church design.

TAKING A BREAK

Try **Atmosphera**, (Panny Marii 3) a light and airy café ideally placed for a pit stop, or the **Kuranty Pub** (Rynek Staromiejski 29), an atmospheric tavern with sunshades out on the square.

✚ 184 C1

Red-brick defensive walls line the riverbank and once surrounded the whole town

Tourist Information Office
✉ Rynek Staromiejski 25 ☎ 056 621 0931; www.it.torun.pl

Copernicus Museum
✉ ul. Kopernika 15/17 ☎ 056 622 7038; www.muzeum.torun.pl ⏱ Summer Tue–Sun 10–6; winter 10–4 💰 Moderate

TORUŃ: INSIDE INFO

Top tip At the information office be sure to ask for the **"Toruń 100 Entries"** guide (1PLN), a small booklet absolutely crammed full of information on events, hotels, tours, eating out and sights, and containing a detailed pull-out transport map and city plan.

Hidden gem One attraction anyone with an interest in Polish folklore should not miss is the local **Ethnographical Museum** (ul. Wały gen. Sikorskiego 19), housing some fascinating historical and contemporary handicrafts and artwork from northern Poland. A small open-air museum of folk architecture surrounds the main building.

5 Poznań

Good transport links, a large student population, thousands of conference tourists and a peppering of undemanding attractions make Poznań feel like a city that's going places. Wielkopolska's major metropolis also played a vital role in the country's history as the birthplace of the Polish nation.

Stary Rynek and Around

The easiest place to start exploring is the impressive **Stary Rynek** (Old Market Square). This busy cobbled expanse, lined with colourful town houses, is dominated by the magnificent Renaissance **town hall**, with its loggia, turrets, lively decoration and tall central tower. Inside, a museum charged with tracing the city's history provides an excuse to nose around the interiors, while outside, the building puts on a show every day at noon involving two mechanical goats who lock horns above the clock to remember the day the animals saved it from a fire. Sadly, they were not around in 1945 when this Renaissance masterpiece was left a smouldering hulk. Next door, the colourful Fish Sellers' Houses line up in an irregular parade. To the south of the Rynek stands the **Church of St Stanisław,** the most elaborate chunk of baroque in town whose adjacent Jesuit college now houses the city's administration. To the west of the Rynek, take a look at the **Franciscan church** in the late baroque style, opposite which lie the anonymous scant remains of **Poznań Castle**.

Plac Wolności and the Western City

Poznań's other piazza is home to the Poznań branch of the **National Museum**, where a rich collection of Polish, Italian, Flemish and Spanish art awaits visitors eyes. The other two

A terrace café at Stary Rynek is the perfect place to eat on a warm summer evening

The Old Market Square is a hive of activity on sunny days

grand buildings here are the 1870 Polish Theatre and the neoclassical Raczyński Library.

Three fascinating attractions lie to the west of Plac Wolności. The **Kaiserhaus** is a prominent reminder that for two centuries Posen (the German name for Poznań) was firmly under Prussian rule. This neo-Romanesque palace was built as a private residence for German Emperor Wilhelm II shortly before Poznań reverted to Polish control in 1919, and is now a large cultural centre and venue. Further along ul. św. Marcin the two colossal crucifixes rising from the pavement form the **Monument to the Victims of June 1956**, the month Poznań was gripped by food riots. One of the crosses bears the years in which key anti-Communist protests took place. Pass through the parkland behind the monument to arrive at the **Grand Theatre**, Poznań's premier opera venue.

Tumski Island

A **cathedral** has occupied Tumski Island for 1,000 years and today's post-World War II rebuild still houses the tomb of Mieszko I, Poland's first ruler. Another highlight is the stunning Renaissance Golden Chapel, and opposite stands **St Mary's**, the oldest church in the city.

TAKING A BREAK

Stary Rynek is awash with cafés in summer, or try the food court at the Stary Browar shopping centre.

➕ 189 E4

Tourist Information Office
✉ ul. Ratajczaka 44 ☎ 061 851 9645; www.poznan.pl 🕐 Mon–Fri 10–7, Sat 10–5

POZNAŃ: INSIDE INFO

Top tip Due to the city's status as a popular international **trade fair destination,** Poznań's hotels can become booked up during big events and room rates are much higher. Be sure to get a bed by booking well ahead.

At Your Leisure

6 Hel

This charming fishing village at the end of a 30km (19-mile) spit of land arching across the Bay of Gdańsk has golden beaches and a small seal sanctuary, but is perhaps more popular for allowing visitors to boast afterwards that they've been to Hel and back. A road and railway track run the length of the sand bank, which narrows to just a few metres in some places and is lined with miles of Baltic sands. An interesting way to reach Hel is by so-called water tram from Gdańsk and Sopot pier. Otherwise it's a scenic drive along the Baltic coast (➤ 170–172). A train also runs direct all the way from Warsaw to Hel via Gdańsk.

⊕ 184 C5

7 Kwidzyn

The only reason to stop in this small town 40km (25 miles) south of Malbork is to admire its hilltop castle and adjacent cathedral, all that survived of a fortified settlement following the ravages of World War II. The mighty red-brick castle, with the spiky gables and steep sloping roofs so typical of northern Poland, was begun by the Teutonic Knights in the 1230s, long before

they plumped for Malbork as their headquarters. The sprawling building is now home to a museum displaying exhibitions of religious art, regional folk handicrafts and the fauna of northern Poland. One unique feature of the building is the former toilet at the top of a separate tower linked to the main building by a long covered walkway. The tower used to stand in the middle of a river, which has long since dried up. Despite several rebuilds, the cathedral retains some of its original Gothic features and is the burial place of local bishops and three Grand Masters of the Teutonic Knights.

⊕ 184 C3
Kwidzyn Castle
✉ ul. Katedralna 1 ☎ 055 646 37 80
🕐 Summer Tue–Sun 9–5; winter 9–3

8 Chełmno

Of all northern Poland's red-brick Gothic towns, sleepy Chełmno, some 40km (25 miles) north along the Vistula from Toruń, is one of the best preserved and well worth a couple of hours to explore its Old Town. This grid of eleven streets with the usual

The village of Hel is popular for its beautiful sandy beaches

View from the belltower of the Assumption of Mary parish church, Chełmno

market square and town hall at the centre is dotted with Gothic churches and is almost completely ringed by a 2.3km (1.5-mile) medieval defensive wall which survived the 19th-century demolition craze, Nazis and Soviets intact. One of the finest buildings is the fairy-tale town hall, a Gothic original wrapped in Renaissance cladding and today housing an interesting museum on the history of the town.

➕ 184 B2
Tourist Information Office
✉ Ratusz-Rynek 28 ☎ 056 686 2104; wwchelmno.pl

St Procopius Church, Strzelno

🕘 Strzelno

Drowsy Strzelno on the Toruń–Poznań road boasts an interesting monastery with many original Romanesque features, if little else. The red sandstone church of St Procopius is one of the best examples of Romanesque church architecture in the country, while the larger Holy Trinity Church bears the marks of later Gothic and baroque makeovers. There's also a small archaeological museum nearby.

➕ 190 B4

🕙 Gniezno

Gniezno has been around since the beginning of the Polish state and played a pivotal role in its birth as the place Poland's first ruler, Duke Mieszko I, was baptised. The now sleepy provincial town could even have grown into Poland's capital had the Piast dynasty not favoured Poznań to the south and then distant Kraków for reasons of security. Gniezno instead grew into a religious centre with an archbishopric established here in 1000. Polish kings were crowned at the cathedral here until the late 13th century, a fact that even modern-day Gnieznians find hard to believe.

Naturally, the focus of attention in Gniezno is the cathedral, somewhat disappointingly a post-war rebuild of the Gothic original, though still a magnificent structure. However, inside you will discover a raft of original tombs and chapels including the sarcophagus of St Adalbert, one of the patron saints of Bohemia (where he is known as St Vojtěch), who was murdered in these parts while trying to convert the pagan Prussians to Christianity in the late 10th century. The cathedral also possesses a pair of original bronze Romanesque doors, a very rare treasure indeed, depicting scenes from the life of St Adalbert.

➕ 189 F5
Cathedral
✉ ul. Łaskiego 9   ☎ 061 424 1389
🕐 Daily 9–5

🔟 Licheń

The gargantuan Basilica of Our Lady at Licheń is the second most significant pilgrimage destination in the country after Częstochowa, attracting almost 1.5 million Catholics a year. Construction was financed solely from donations and the church was conceived on a massive scale; not only is it Poland's highest, and widest, it is also the 11th longest in the world! The two features that stand out most prominently from the outside are the huge gilt cupola and the almost free-standing belfry in which hangs one of the biggest bells in the country. When tired of the superlatives on the outside, head into the church to see the miracle-working icon of the Virgin Mary, the humble image that draws the devout in such great numbers. The rest of the inside is awash with gilt decoration and confessionals, and there are interesting exhibitions on religious themes held near the underground Golden Chapel.

➕ 182 C1   ✉ ul. Klasztorna 4, Lichen Stary
🕐 Daily 5:30am–10:30pm

🔢 Kórnik

Dinky, moat-encircled Kórnik Castle, half an hour's drive south of Poznań, was completed in around 1430 as the Gothic residence of the Górka family. Graced by Polish royalty and celebrity over the centuries, Kórnik was transformed in stages by various aristocratic owners from Gothic residence to defensive fort to baroque palace, ultimately gaining its current mock-Gothic appearance in the mid-19th century. This final rebuild was undertaken by Tytus

Small-scale Kórnik Castle

Charming Rogalin Palace is surrounded by extensive parkland

Działyński, whose family had owned Kórnik since 1676. Władysław Zamoyski, the castle's last owner and great Polish patriot, turned it over to the state in 1924 as a gift to the resurrected nation.

From the outside the thickset chateau, accessed by a neo-Gothic footbridge, looks like two buildings merging into one another. Inside, the rooms on the ground floor boast wonderfully intricate inlaid parquet floors, imposing carved doorways, antique furniture collected by Władysław Zamoyski and the Działyński family and magnificent coffered ceilings. One room is even home to a piano which Chopin is said to have played. The real highlight of the castle, however, comes upstairs where Tytus Działyński created an Alhambra-inspired Mauritanian Hall resplendent with snow-white Moorish columns and archways elaborately carved with symmetrical Islamic designs.

🚩 189 E4 ✉ Zamkowa 5 ☎ 061 817 0081
🕐 Summer Tue–Sun 9–5:30; winter until 3:30

🔢 Rogalin

This sweeping palace surrounded by verdant parkland can be visited in combination with Kórnik 15km (9 miles) away on a long day trip out of Poznań. Built in 1768 by wealthy nobleman, Kazimierz Raczyński, this horseshoe of neoclassical grandeur remained the family's prize possession until World War II. The last owner, Edward Raczyński, served as Polish President in Exile in London in the early 1980s.

Approached via a grand alley of mature horse chestnut trees, the perfectly symmetrical ochre-and-white palace is a truly regal sight. Sadly, only a small portion of the interior is open to the public, including a mock-up of Edward Raczyński's London apartment, several rooms which re-create period interiors (Empire study, Louis XVI-style parlour) and the orangery created from the 18th-century chapel. Perhaps the highlight of any visit to Rogalin is Edward Raczyński's gallery which exhibits a superb collection of paintings by such Polish greats as Matejko, Wyspiański, Bożnańska and Malczewski. Five minutes' walk from the palace stands the Raczyński Mausoleum where Edward Raczyński is buried, and in the grounds you will also find three fantastically gnarled millennium-old oaks named Lech, Rus and Czech after the mythical founders of Poland, Russia and Bohemia. The palace is currently undergoing a thorough renovation and is not expected to re-open until mid-2009.

🚩 189 E4 ☎ 061 813 8030; www.rogalin.eu
💲 Moderate

Where to... Stay

Prices

Expect to pay per night for a double room (in peak season):

€ under 200PLN €€ 200PLN–500PLN €€€ over 500PLN

GDAŃSK

Kamienica Gotyk €€

There is no more central place to stay in Gdańsk than this six-room hotel at the end of Mariacka Street, housed in what the owners claim to be the oldest house in Gdańsk. Rooms are small but the little touches such as stained glass and Gothic arched doorways make up for that. Reserve well ahead.

🚹 184 C4 ☒ ul. Mariacka 1 ☎ 058 301 8567; www.gotykhouse.eu

Podewils €€€

Occupying a residence built in the 1720s on the opposite side of the River Motława to the city centre, the bijou Podewils is one of Gdańsk's finest hotels. Its five-star rating is justified by faultless service, understated style and plush rooms equipped with marble bathrooms, DVD players and flat-screen TVs. There's an excellent restaurant, secure parking and a sauna. There are only ten rooms, so reserve early.

🚹 184 C4 ☒ ul. Szafarnia 2 ☎ 058 300 9560; www.podewils.pl

MALBORK

Hotel Stary Malbork €€

The vast majority of people visit Malbork as a daytrip from Gdansk, but if you do decide to stay in the town, the Stary Malbork is arguably the most comfortable option. Easily spotted from the outside by its double castle-like turrets and pastel green facade, inside you'll find 25 simply furnished, clean rooms that do the job for a night or two. Prices include breakfast.

🚹 184 C3 ☒ ul. 17 Marca 26-27 ☎ 055 647 2400; www.hotelstarymalbork.com.pl

POZNAŃ

Młyńskie Koło €€

The "Mill Wheel" is by no means your run-of-the-mill hotel with its antique-strewn guestrooms housed in a large log-built lodge. The popular restaurant of the same name serves up countryside portions of forest wildlife in a suitably timber environment. Although some distance from the city centre it's worth the extra effort to get here.

🚹 189 E4 ☒ ul. Browarna 37 ☎ 061 878 9935; www.mlynskiekolo.pl

Rezydent €€€

In their rush to stay at the beach, many might overlook this luxurious hotel on a pretty square at the top of the main drag. The Rezydent has sumptuous five-star guestrooms with every facility you can imagine and a top-rate restaurant, all just a ten-minute walk from the pier.

🚹 184 C4 ☒ Plac Konstytucji 3 Maja 3 ☎ 058 555 5800; www.hotelrezydent.pl

SOPOT

TORUŃ

Spichrz €€

Toruń's best hotel occupies a historical 18th-century granary on the banks of the Vistula. The inside has received a modern refit, though rooms still have the original hefty wooden beams and timber ceilings. Some enjoy scenic river views. The on-site Karczma restaurant is a rural affair serving a country menu.

🚹 184 C1 ☒ ul. Mostowa 1 ☎ 056 657 1140; www.spichrz.pl

Where to...
Eat and Drink

Prices
Expect to pay for a three-course meal for one, excluding drinks:
€ under 50PLN €€ 50PLN–100PLN €€€ over 100PLN

GDAŃSK

Gdańska
Dining at Gdańsk's best known restaurant is like eating at a museum within a church, so bedecked are its five halls with stained glass, high-backed ornately carved chairs, oil paintings, antiques, baroque mirrors, chandeliers and Persian rugs. The food suits the environment with huge helpings of fish, duck, goose, Polish pork and other serious belly-fillers delivered to your overdressed table by scurrying waiters. Despite the formal appearance, it's OK to turn up in fleece and walking shoes.
☐ 184 C4 ⬛ ul. Św. Ducha 16/24 ☏ 058 305 7671 ⏱ Daily 11am–midnight

Kresowa €€
This delightful restaurant, which lies slightly off the beaten tourist trail, is well worth seeking out for its old-world charm and perfectly balanced menu of Polish, Russian, Ukrainian, Lithuanian and Jewish dishes. Feast on platters of *pelmeni*, dumplings, chicken Kiev, *bigos*, veal and venison served by waitresses in traditional garb at beautifully laid

tables either downstairs or upstairs in the mirrored dining room. Jewish and Polish music enhance the already magical ambience.
☐ 184 C4 ⬛ ul. Ogarna 12 ☏ 058 301 6653 ⏱ Daily 11am–last customer

Targ Rybny €€–€€€
It's not difficult to guess what the main component of the menu is going to be in a restaurant whose name translates as "the fish market". Standing on what was once Gdańsk's own fish market, this sometimes pricey eatery has a light wood interior and tables with chequered tablecloths at which you can enjoy inhabitants of the Baltic and more distant seas. The perfect place to dine for fish lovers.
☐ 184 C4 ⬛ ul. Targ Rybny 6C ☏ 058 320 9011 ⏱ Daily 11–11

MALBORK

Piwniczka
Located inside the castle itself, this Gothic tavern with its vaulting

overhead, flagstones under foot and dark wood tables and benches is an atmospheric place to eat, in keeping with a tour of the castle. The English-language menu is weighed down with mock Polish medieval fare, which comes in belly-busting portions. It's OK when half full, but this place (and its staff) can be sometimes overwhelmed by tour bus groups on a feeding frenzy.
☐ 184 C3 ⬛ ul Starościńska 1 (castle) ☏ 055 273 3668 ⏱ Daily 11–10

POZNAŃ

Brovaria
One of Poznań's most fashionable wining and dining venues, this sometimes hectic microbrewery and restaurant complex on the main square allows visitors to choose from a 14m-long (15-yard) bar, an intimate cellar space, a dining room with views of the old square below and a cavernous hall where shiny vats and tubes used in the brewing process can be observed in action

while tucking into top-notch soak-up material for the three types of ale fermented on the premises. For those who don't fancy a beer there's an extensive cocktail menu.

⊞ 189 E4 ⊠ Stary Rynek 73/74
☎ 061 858 6868 ⏰ Daily 11am–1am

Pod Dzwonkiem €€

A short walk from the Stary Rynek you'll discover this rural themed restaurant with chunky timber beams, chairs made of old barrels, rough whitewashed walls and a menu of traditional rural fare such as tripe soup, duck breast in apple and plum sauce and pear in cheese and chocolate sauce. There's Czech and Polish beer on tap to wash it all down, as well as a large choice of vodkas.

⊞ 189 E4 ⊠ ul. Garbary 54 ☎ 061 851 9970 ⏰ Daily noon–10pm

Ratuszowa €–€€

Another central eatery, this time a more traditional affair beneath the town hall with a meat-orientated

menu and bags of character-squeezed into rambling brick cellar. This place has been serving Poznań's peckish for 50 years so it must be doing something right.

⊞ 189 E4 ⊠ Stary Rynek 55 ☎ 061 851 0513 ⏰ Daily noon–11pm

SOPOT

Błękitny Pudel €

Little prepares you for the riot of antiques and knick-knacks that litter Sopot's most characterful eatery, easy to find opposite the Krzywy Dom. You'll discover some new bit of intriguing junk every time you step across the threshold, but if you can take your gaze away from the interior long enough, you may also find the very reasonably priced Polish fare on offer.

⊞ 184 C4 ⊠ Bohaterów Monte Cassino 44 ☎ 058 551 1672 ⏰ Daily 10am–midnight

Koliba €–€€

This faux highland tavern may look slightly out of place just a few steps

off the beach west of Sopot centre, but its incongruous appearance is soon forgotten when you sit down to a hearty meal or a beer inside. By day this is a pleasant lunch or dinner spot, but on summer weekend evenings the volume is turned up, the furniture pushed back and the place turns into a beachside disco.

⊞ 184 C4 ⊠ ul. Powstańców Warszawy
⏰ Daily 24 hours

TORUŃ

Gęsia Szyja €

This busy and extremely popular first-floor restaurant, with an atmospheric backstreet location just off ul. Szeroka, sees diners off the urban streets straight into an oversize rural cottage packed with antique dressers, wicker lampshades and solid timber tables. There are even mock log walls and windows with two-dimensional rural views to complete the effect. As you would expect, the menu is

heavy with country fare, though you could just plump for a quick *zapiekanka* and a pint. It's chock-a-block here at mealtimes – always a good sign.

⊞ 184 C1 ⊠ ul. Podmurna 28
☎ 056 621 1249
⏰ Sun–Wed noon–midnight, Thu–Sat noon–1am

Zaczarowana Dorożka €€

The "Enchanted Coach" can be found opposite the Cathedral of St John the Baptist and just a few steps off the main drag. While the interior is a bit spartan and not the most exciting you'll see in Poland, the emphasis here is off gimmicky decor and firmly on honest, well cooked food with a Polish and Mediterranean accent. The menu lists a greater number of fish options than is usual and there is a good selection of filling meat dishes, *pierogi*, soups and salads to choose from.

⊞ 184 C1 ⊠ ul. Łazienna 24
☎ 056 621 1401 ⏰ Daily 1–11

Where to... Shop

AMBER

Although it's available across Poland and, indeed, across Eastern Europe, Poland's north coast is the place to pick up some "Baltic Gold". Buying it from the sea where it is found seems better than getting it from a stall in Southern Poland or Warsaw, and the choice in Gdańsk is far superior to any other town in the land. The best places to head are the many stalls and boutiques in Mariacka Street, Długa Street and Długi Targ where several outlets sell everything from dainty earrings to chunky necklaces. Amber is incredibly easy to fake in plastic or even sugar, so beware making purchases from makeshift street stalls. There are ways of ascertaining whether a piece is real which involve burning, licking and scratching, none of which is likely to endear you with Gdańsk's shopkeepers. Never buy anything that looks too perfect or large shiny pieces with bargain basement price tags.

GOLDWASSER

Gdańsk's other signature souvenir is Goldwasser, a 40% proof herbal liqueur containing real flakes of gold leaf which swirl around and sparkle when the bottle is shaken. Gold was once believed to have medicinal properties and hence flakes were first added to alcohol in the 18th century. Gold has no adverse effects on the body and swallowing a few flecks will do you no harm at all. Goldwasser is available in specialist shops in Gdańsk as well as every supermarket and souvenir shop across the land and makes an interesting gift.

GINGERBREAD

Continuing the golden theme, when in Toruń be sure to try the town's famous gingerbread. This comes in a multitude of chocolate coated, jam-filled sizes and traditional designs including carriages, coats of arms, knights, townsfolk at work, hearts and a sort of cloud shape called a *Katarzynka*. The sweet treat is still made according to a medieval recipe and if you want to buy some, the best shops are the **Dwór Artusa** on the main square, **Emporium** (ul. Piekary 28) and **Pierniczek** (ul. Żeglarska 25).

STARY BROWAR SHOPPING MALL

Poznań's huge, award-winning shopping mall housed in a red-brick former brewery is one of the northwest's premier retail experiences with three distinct areas (The Atrium, The Courtyard of Art and The Passage) accommodating 100 shops and restaurants and an exhibition area. Located within walking distance of the city centre.

CEPELIA

The Polish national chain of local handicraft and art shops has three outlets in Gdańsk (ul. Grunwaldzka 31, ul. Długa 47 and ul. Jagiellońska 10) and three in Poznań (ul. Woźna 12, ul. Ratajczaka 20 and ul. Klasztorna 62) selling their typical selection of authentic locally produced items.

MALBORK

As the castle at Malbork lures tourists by the coachload, it's quite a good place to pick up souvenirs, though here they tend to be on the tackier side. The Teutonic Knights seem to be the overriding theme on the stalls near the castle.

Where to...
Be Entertained

CLASSICAL MUSIC, OPERA AND BALLET

The **Baltic Opera** (www.operabaltycka.pl) and the **Polish Baltic Philharmonic** (www.filharmonia.gda.pl) take care of cultural entertainment in the Tri-City area. The Poznań Philharmonic (www.filharmonia.poznan.pl) do the same in Wielkopolska. Sopot's **Opera Leśna** (Forest Opera) is a regular summer concert venue as well as hosting an international song contest. Poznań also has a respectable opera and ballet venue in the shape of the **Teatr Wielki** (Grand Theatre, www.opera.poznan.pl).

SOPOT INTERNATIONAL SONG FESTIVAL

Almost every year since 1961 this famous song contest and megaconcert has taken place at the Forest Opera to the west of town. It was once a showcase for Eastern Bloc talent, but since the fall of communism stars such as Vanessa Mae, The Village People, Elton John and Dannii Minogue have performed at the August even..

FESTIVALS

Gdansk's **Jarmark Św. Dominika** (St. Dominic's Fair, www.mtgsz.pl) is the city's biggest event and takes place over three weeks in Augu.st.

The streets of the main town are packed with hundreds of antiques and second-hand stalls, and there are pop and rock concerts, folk performances, firework displays and sporting tournaments to entertain the estimated 150,000 people who attend the fair every day. Gdansk also hosts the annual **Feta Festival** (mid-July), a street theatre festival. Poznań holds a **jazz festival** in March and the **Malta Theatre Festival** (www.malta-festival.pl) in June as well as several smaller events throughout the year. The major annual events in Toruń are the **Probaltica Music and Art Festival** in May (www.probaltica.art.pl) and the **Music and Architecture Festival** held from June to August.

WATER SPORTS

The Baltic coast is a mecca for anyone who likes water sports. Sailing, windsurfing, swimming, diving and all manner of other zany pursuits are possible, and there is a raft of companies in the Tri-City area willing to loan you the equipment and show you the ropes.

CINEMA

Gdansk's **City Krewetka** (ul. Karmelicka 1), Poznań's **Kinepolis** (ul. Bolesława Krzywoustego 72) and Toruń's **Cinema City** (ul. Czerwona Droga 1) are the pick of the region's cinemas.

NIGHTLIFE

Sopot is the summer nightclub capital of Poland, with a string of innovative theme bars and cool clubs extending from the town and out along the dunes.

WHAT'S ON

Gdańsk and Poznań are large enough to warrant their very own *In Your Pocket Guides*. Otherwise ask at the local tourist office.

Walks and Tours

WARSAW HISTORICAL CENTRE

Walk

1

This classic linear walking route follows the Royal Way from the university quarter on Krakowskie Przedmieście to the Citadel via many of the city's most attractive works of architecture, picturesque squares and atmospheric cobbled lanes. There are many opportunities to leave the route to explore churches, town walls and monuments along the way, as well as to admire views across the River Vistula. This is the most popular tour taken by almost every visitor to the Polish capital so unless you try it at 3am, you are unlikely to have the streets to yourself.

1–2

Start your exploration at the crossroads of ul. Świętokrzyska Krakowskie Przedmieście and Nowy Świat. Immediately on the right you will notice the **statue of Copernicus** (Pomnik Kopernika) past which students scurry to lectures at the nearby **university**. This former Royal

DISTANCE 6km (4 miles)
TIME Half-day or whole day, depending on stops at places of interest along the way
START POINT Krakowskie Przedmieście 🚼 198 C3 **END POINT** Citadel 🚼 199 D5

Way is lined with churches and palaces but only some can be visited. First of all, pop in to the **Church of the Holy Cross** (Kościół św Krzyża) to see Chopin's heart, then continue to the **Bristol Hotel** (right) behind which

stands the **Pałac Radziwiłłów**, scene of many great events in Polish history. Almost opposite the main tourist information office rises the impressive white facade of the

Statue of Copernicus, the famous astronomer

the **Royal Castle** (Zamek Królewski). Take time out of the walk if you wish to do the castle's tour. Beyond the castle lies Warsaw's bijoux Old Town (Stare Miasto), a tight-knit grid of cobbled streets crammed full of cafés and shops. Ul. Świętojańska is perhaps the most interesting route through the area as it is graced by the red-brick Gothic facade of **St John's Cathedral** (Katedra św Jana) and a Jesuit church, both of which can be entered free of charge. Ul. Świętojańska will also take you directly from Plac Zamkowy to Warsaw's piece de resistance and tourist magnet, the wonderful **Old Town Square** (Rynek Starego Miasta). This is one of the best places along the way to grab a drink before exploring the Warsaw History Museum on its northern flank and admiring the miraculous restoration carried out in the post-war years.

Church of St Anne (Kościół św Anny), where you can take a quick scramble up the belfry to observe the rest of your route from above.

2–3

From the Church of St Anne it's just a few steps to the triangular Plac Zamkowy dominated by the dark pink building of

Taking a Break

This entire walk is lined with some of Warsaw's finest cafés, bars and restaurants and you can stop almost anywhere en route for refreshment, though options are limited towards the end near the citadel.

Map labels:
Wisła
Kościół Sakramentek pod wezwaniem św Kazimierza
Muzeum Marii Skłodowskiej-Curie
Rynek Starego Miasta **3**
Katedra św Jana
Barbakan Boleść
Zamek Królewski
Grodzka
WYBRZEŻE GDAŃSKIE
MOST ŚLĄSKO DĄBROWSKI
Clasi... Kozla Freta Świętojańska Piwna Podwale pl Zamkowy **2**
Pomnik Powstania Warszawskiego
Długa STARE MIASTO
Katedra Polowa Wojska Polskiego **4**
Schillera Miodowa Senatorska
Kościół św Anny
Pałac Radziwiłłów
MARIENSZAT
Bristol Hotel
Karowa Karowa
Dobra
Gęsta
Browarna Lipowa
Obozna
Krakowskie Przedmieście
Uniwersytet Warszawski
Pomnik Kopernika
Mollera
Ossolińskich
pl Teatralny
Bielańska Wierzbowa Niecała
Ogród Saski
Królewska
Kredytowa
Świętokrzyska
R Traugutta
Kościół św Krzyża
NOWY ŚWIAT **1**
Świętojerska
Bon Cetta
Krasińskich
Ogród Krasiński **4**
Ratusz Arsenal
pl Bankowy
CEN WŁ A...
Senatorska
500 m
500 yds
0
0

3–4

From the city's most appealing piazza, make your way north along ul. Freta to the **Barbakan**, the only surviving gate in the town walls. From here you can branch off to explore the red-brick defences, which run in a semicircle back to Plac Zamkowy, or push on out of the Old Town. Fight the urge to carry on in a straight line with the crowds and take a left into ul. Długa where you'll discover the Polish **Army Field Cathedral** (Katedra Polowa Wojska Polskiego). The anchor and propeller in front of the cathedral are symbols of the armed forces with which it has been associated since 1920. At the end of the street the striking **Warsaw Uprising Monument** (Pomnik Powstania Warzawskiego) commemorates the 1944 uprising against the Nazis with bronze soldiers emerging from the sewers and charging forward, rifles in hand. Retrace your steps to rejoin the main route.

4–5

Ul. Novomiejska passes the **Maria Skłodowska-Curie Museum** on its way to the New Town

A horse and carriage ride is a fun way for tourists to see the sights of the Old Town

Square (Rynek Nowego Miasta). There's nothing new about the New Town, which was founded in the late 14th century, though it was not returned to its former glory after the destruction of 1945 and leaves a less striking impression. The only building of note on the square is the **Church of the Nuns of the Holy Sacrament** (Kościól Sakramentek pod wezwaniem św Kazimierza).

5–6

The majority of strollers turn back at the **New Town Square** but it is worth continuing for another 500m (545 yards) to reach the **Citadel** (Cytadela), a huge 19th-century fortress built by the Russians during their occupation of Eastern Poland following the Partitions. It was put to use by the Tsarist authorities as a political prison, and a museum preserves some of the cells and tells the story of some of the most prominent Polish prisoners incarcerated here. To return to the city centre, take the metro from Dworzec Gdański or bus 175 from just south of the Citadel.

This emotive monument was erected to commemorate the **Warsaw uprising in 1944**

2 KRAKÓW HISTORICAL CENTRE

Walk

DISTANCE 2km (1 mile)
TIME At least 3 hours excluding a tour of Wawel Hill
START POINT Barbican ✚ 200 B5 **END POINT** Grunwaldzki Bridge ✚ 200 A2

This classic route will take you all the way through Kraków's Old Town from the Barbican in the north to the Vistula River in the south via the Rynek and Wawel Hill.

1–2

Your exploration of Kraków's glorious historical core starts at the **Barbakan** in the north, a hefty red-brick gate built in 1498 to beef up the city's defences and along with the walls and Florian Gate in front virtually the only section to have survived 19th-century demolition. The **Florian Gate** (Brama Floriańska) which stands in front of the Barbican, is older and dates from the 14th century. Pass through the gate, but instead of heading into the thick of things in ul. Floriańska, take a right into quieter ul. Św. Jana. Here you will find the The **Czartoryski Museum** (Muzeum Książąt Czartoryszkich),

Kraków's top art display housed in the Czartoryski Palace (▶82). From the museum, head along ul. Św. Jana past various bars and restaurants then turn left into ul. Św Marka which leads back to ul. Floriańska. Turn right and you'll already have the **Rynek Główny** in your sights, but don't rush as this pedestrian thoroughfare is one of Kraków's prettiest and busiest, and is lined with upmarket boutiques, fast-food outlets, several hotels and some interesting restaurants and pubs.

2–3

At the end of ul. Floriańska the Rynek Główny, Kraków's most celebrated public space, spreads out in front of you. Always alive with tourists, stalls, open-air

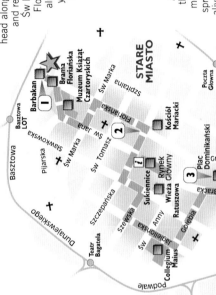

exhibitions, street performers and café tables, this is one of Europe's finest piazzas. It was also its biggest when established in the 14th century, though it was soon overtaken. To your left rises the asymmetrical **Church of St Mary** (Kościól Mariacki), which stands at an odd angle to the rest of the square. If you're lucky you'll arrive on the hour to hear the *hejnat*, a bugle call played to announce the opening and closing of the city gates and to warn of fires and other dangers. After inspecting the church's overwhelmingly rich interior it's just a few steps across the cobbles to the Rynek's other architectural masterpiece, the **Cloth Hall** (Sukiennice). This huge Renaissance structure dominates the Rynek's centre and attracts visitors with its indoor souvenir market and art gallery. Its sole rival for attention is the **Town Hall Tower** (Wieża Ratuszowa), which rises 70m (230 feet) over the square and is all that remains of a town hall demolished by the Austrians in 1820.

You could spend hours discovering all the façades, shops, restaurants and cafés on the

The 14th-century Florian Gate towers over the bustling crowds on ul. Florianska

Rynek and the stories behind them, but once you've had your fill of medieval grandeur here, resist the temptation to go with the tourist flow and leave the square to the south, instead taking ul. Szewska on the western flank until it meets Jagiellońska, where you should turn left. On the right you will discover the Collegium Maius, the oldest university building in Poland dating from the 15th century. Tours of the original interiors leave every half an hour. From the Collegium Maius take ul. Gołębia to ul. Bracka, at the end of which stands the Franciscan Church, which is closely associated with Pope John Paul II. Candles are kept burning outside 24-hours a day in his memory. You've now reached **Plac Dominikański** whose length is scored by tramlines. Dodge the trams and follow the throngs into ul. Grodzka.

3–4

Ul. Grodzka which could be regarded as a continuation of ul. Floriańska south of the Rynek, though its shops and restaurants have a slightly earthier feel. This busy street will take you to the foot of Wawel Hill but there

The Sukiennice (Cloth Hall) in Rynek Glowny Town Square is an architectural masterpiece

are a couple of essential stops along the way. On the left two striking places of worship, the baroque **Church of SS Peter and Paul** (Kościół św Piotra i Pawła), with a gallery of statues lining its entrance, and the Romanesque **Church of St Andrew** (Kościól św Andrzeja) next door, with its the twin towers and bare stone facades, present a real contrast in styles. Ul. Grodzka eventually peters out at the cobbled slope leading up to **Wawel Castle** (Palac Kroleski na Wawelu) and **Wawel Cathedral** (Katedra Wawelska).

4–5

Books as thick as this guide could be, and indeed have been, written about the complex of buildings that sit atop Wawel Hill. The castle, cathedral and numerous exhibitions take almost a full day to see and should not be rushed. Our target is the lift at the southwestern corner of the ramparts, which takes visitors down to the Dragon's Cave. Not only is this an interesting route off Wawel Hill, it's also the quickest way of descending to the Vistula.

The pleasant walk south along the riverbank is a relaxing way to end your tour and brings you to the **Grunwaldzki Bridge** from where trams return to the centre.

An impressive view across Vistula river to Wawel Castle, in Kraków

3 ALONG THE BALTIC COAST

Drive

DISTANCE 210km (130 miles)
TIME At least a day
START POINT Gdańsk ⊞ 184 C4 **END POINT** Słowiński National Park ⊞ 183 F5

The stretch of coastline from Gdańsk to the Słowiński National Park takes drivers out of the city suburbs via nightlife spots, industrial heritage and fishing communities to one of the most distinctive national parks in the country.

1–2

Head out of Gdańsk along the main Grunwaldzka dual carriageway through the northern suburbs to your first stop, the seaside resort of **Sopot** with its lively Bohaterów Monte Cassino Street and Europe's longest wooden pier. After a stroll to the water's edge, an ice cream and, if the weather is very hot, a quick dip in the Baltic, it's back on the road.

2–3

The Tri-City's main transport artery eventually brings you to the poor relation in the trio, the

Relax on the beautiful sandy beach at Hel and take a dip in the Baltic Sea

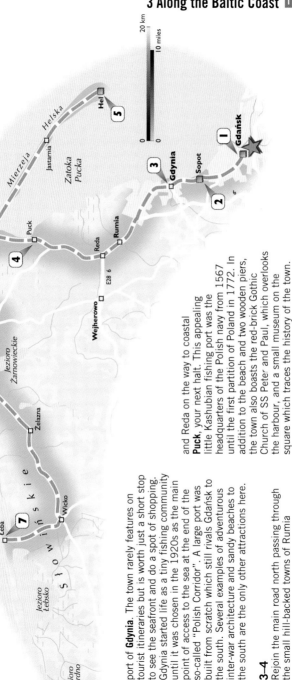

port of **Gdynia**. The town rarely features on tourist itineraries but is worth just a short stop to see the seafront and do a spot of shopping. Gdynia started life as a tiny fishing community until it was chosen in the 1920s as the main point of access to the sea at the end of the so-called "Polish Corridor". A large port was built from scratch which still rivals Gdańsk to the south. Several examples of adventurous inter-war architecture and sandy beaches to the south are the only other attractions here.

3–4
Rejoin the main road north passing through the small hill-backed towns of Rumia

and Reda on the way to coastal **Puck**, your next halt. This appealing little Kashubian fishing port was the headquarters of the Polish navy from 1567 until the first partition of Poland in 1772. In addition to the beach and two wooden piers, the town also boasts the red-brick Gothic Church of SS Peter and Paul, which overlooks the harbour, and a small museum on the square which traces the history of the town.

the roundabout at Władysławowo go straight on. This coastal road will bring you to the peaceful resort of **Jastrzębia Góra**, where high sandy cliffs afford wide-reaching views out to the ocean. The beaches are the principal draw here, and when you've caught enough rays you can take a relaxing stroll in the forests behind the village. Jastrzębia Góra has a disproportionate number of restaurants and cafés for its size and is another good place to call a lunch halt.

6–7

From Jastrzębia Góra you can either pick your way through the system of tiny country lanes along the coast or head inland onto route 213. The latter will take you past Lake Żarnowieckie and through several pretty Kashubian villages to a crossroads where you should turn right back towards the coast. End of the line here is the town of **Łeba** (pronounced "Weba"), a fine Baltic resort with miles of dunes, beaches and forests lining the coast in both directions. Łeba is also the gateway to the **Słowiński National Park** 1.5km (1 mile) away. Here, picturesque beaches and shifting dunes, reaching almost 40m (131 feet) high protect two lagoons called Łebsko and Gardno from the Baltic's storms.

Boats rest in the calm harbour at Hel on the north coast of the peninsula

35km-long (22-mile) thin spit of sand which protrudes into the Bay of Gdańsk is a fascinating place to explore, and it is worth stopping on the road to **Hel** to admire the sandy beaches. At some points the peninsula is just a few metres wide, at others it can support a whole village. One such settlement is Jastarnia, an excellent place to take a break. Try Café Marta, which specialises in Kashubian cuisine. After Jastarnia the peninsula widens out slightly and the woods thicken as you approach the end of the road and the village of Hel. The main attractions here are the beach and a small seal sanctuary where visitors can get very close to the animals who normally swim the open waters of the Baltic. In summer, Hel welcomes hundreds of tourists a day, many of whom come from Gdańsk and Sopot by boat or arrive from further afield by rail.

5–6

Unfortunately there's only one way out of Hel and that's back the way you came. Retrace your route back along the peninsula, but at

4–5

The road now hugs the coast as far as Władysławowo, where you should take a right at the roundabout onto the road which runs the length of the Hel Peninsula. This

Practicalities

BEFORE YOU GO

WHAT YOU NEED

		UK	Germany	USA	Canada	Australia	Ireland	Netherlands	Spain
● Required ○ Suggested ▲ Not required	Some countries require a passport to remain valid for a minimum period (usually at least six months) beyond the date of entry – check before booking								
Passport/National Identity Card		●	●	●	●	●	●	●	●
Visa (regulations can change – check before booking)		▲	▲	▲	▲	▲	▲	▲	▲
Onward or Round-Trip Ticket		○	○	○	○	○	○	○	○
Health Inoculations (tetanus and polio)		▲	▲	▲	▲	▲	▲	▲	▲
Health Documentation (▶ 178, Health)		▲	▲	▲	▲	▲	▲	▲	▲
Travel Insurance		○	○	○	○	○	○	○	○
Driver's Licence (national)		●	●	●	●	●	●	●	●
Car Insurance Certificate		●	●	●	●	●	●	●	●
Car Registration Document		●	●	●	●	●	●	●	●

WHEN TO GO

Peak season   Off-season

JAN	FEB	MAR	APR	MAY	JUN	JUL	AUG	SEP	OCT	NOV	DEC
0°C	-3°C	2°C	8°C	14°C	18°C	20°C	19°C	15°C	9°C	4°C	0°C
32°F	27°F	36°F	46°F	57°F	64°F	68°F	66°F	59°F	48°F	39°F	32°F

Very wet Wet Cloud Sun Sun/Showers

The temperatures shown above are the average daily maximum for each month for central Poland. Conditions on the Baltic coast and in the mountainous regions of the south differ. Gdańsk normally experiences higher winter temperatures than central regions but lower summer values; temperatures in the mountains are on average around 10°C (50°F) lower. Southern regions experience much greater rainfall in the summer months than the Baltic coast. The best times of year to visit are spring and autumn to avoid the worst of the summer heat, crowds and mosquitos (and the winter chill). Of course, the best months for skiing are from December to March and to get a tan on the Baltic coast it's best to arrive in high season (July and August). The busiest times are July, August and Christmas, especially in Kraków. Some tourist attractions close down from November to April.

GETTING ADVANCE INFORMATION

Websites
Polish Tourist Board:
www.poland.travel/en/
Polish web portal:
www.poland.pl

Ministry of Foreign Affairs
(visa information):
www.msz.gov.pl
Online rail information:
www.pkp.pl

**Polish Tourist Offices
In the UK**
✉ Westgate House, West Gate, London W5 1YY
☎ 08700 675 010

GETTING THERE

By Air International airports can be found in Warsaw, Kraków, Gdańsk, Wrocław, Poznań, Łódź, Rzeszów, Szczecin, Bydgoszcz and Katowice. The Polish national airline LOT operates a scheduled service from Warsaw to most major cities in Europe and a handful in the US and Canada, with flights from other destinations in North America and around the world available through the Star Alliance network. Poland is very well served by budget airlines such as Ryanair, easyJet, bmibaby, Centralwings and Wizz Air. The majority of European national airlines operate flights to Warsaw.

By Land Poland shares land borders with Germany, Russia (Kaliningrad Enclave), Lithuania, Belarus, Ukraine, Slovakia and the Czech Republic. There are direct coach connections to major cities in Western Europe with many bus services operating to and from every major centre in the UK. Rail links Poland with Germany and other countries in central and Eastern Europe and is sometimes quicker and less hassle than flying.

By Sea Ferries operated by Stena Line and Polferries operate between the Baltic coast and Scandinavia (Denmark and Sweden).

TIME

Poland is on Central European Time (CET), one hour ahead of Greenwich Mean Time (GMT). Summer time (GMT+2) operates from the last Sunday in March until the last Sunday in October.

CURRENCY AND FOREIGN EXCHANGE

Currency The traditional Polish currency since medieval times has been the złoty (abbreviated to zł or PLN), which literally means "gold". One złoty is divided into 100 groszy. Notes come in denominations of 10, 20, 50, 100 and 200 złoty, coins come in 1, 2, 5, 10, 20 and 50 groszy and 1, 2 and 5 złoty values. Euros can be used to pay for goods and services at a limited number of shops and hotels but expect exchange rates to be poor. Poland is not expected to join the eurozone any time soon.

Exchange Change foreign currency for złoty at the numerous *kantors* (desks or small kiosks) which have superior rates to banks. Travellers' cheques can only be cashed at banks and some hotels. Withdrawing cash from ATMs is more convenient than using travellers' cheques, but you'll need to know your PIN (Personal Identification Number) and not all Polish ATMs take all cards. Inform your bank before you leave home that you intend making withdrawals in Poland. Banks charge a fee for using ATMs abroad.

Credit and Debit Cards
Card use is on the increase but Poland essentially still has a cash culture.

In the US
✉ 5 Marine View Plaza,
Hoboken, NJ 07030-5722
☎ 201/420-9910

In France
✉ 9 rue de la Paix, 75002
Paris ☎ 01 42 44 19 00

In Germany
✉ Kurfürstendamm 71,
10709 Berlin
☎ 030 210 0920

WHEN YOU ARE THERE

CLOTHING SIZES

UK	Italy	USA	
36	46	36	Suits
38	48	38	
40	50	40	
42	52	42	
44	54	44	
46	56	46	
7	41	8	Shoes
7.5	42	8.5	
8.5	43	9.5	
9.5	44	10.5	
10.5	45	11.5	
11	46	12	
14.5	37	14.5	Shirts
15	38	15	
15.5	39/40	15.5	
16	41	16	
16.5	42	16.5	
17	43	17	
8	34	6	Dresses
10	36	8	
12	38	10	
14	40	12	
16	42	14	
18	44	16	
4.5	38	6	Shoes
5	38	6.5	
5.5	39	7	
6	39	7.5	
6.5	40	8	
7	41	8.5	

NATIONAL HOLIDAYS

1 Jan	New Year's Day
Mar/Apr	Easter Monday
1 May	Labour Day
3 May	Constitution Day
May/Jun	Corpus Christi
15 Aug	Assumption Day
1 Nov	All Saints' Day
11 Nov	Independence Day
25 Dec	Christmas Day
26 Dec	Second Day of Christmas

OPENING HOURS

- ○ Stores
- ● Offices
- ● Banks
- ● Post Offices
- ● Museums/Monuments
- ● Pharmacies

8am 9am 10am noon 1pm 2pm 4pm 5pm 7pm

☐ Day   ▨ Midday   ☐ Evening

Shops Small grocery stores open early and close late, and there is usually one 24-hour shop in every town or district. Most small shops close around 2pm on Saturdays and many remain shut on Sunday. Large supermarkets and city malls are open every day.
Banks Most close on Saturdays at 1pm or 2pm and Sundays.
Places of interest There are no hard and fast rules about opening times when it comes to tourist attractions such as museums and galleries. The vast majority close on Monday.
Pharmacies At least one in every town remains open 24 hours, even at weekends.
Post offices In large cities the main post office may stay open until 10pm.

TIME DIFFERENCES

GMT
12 noon

Poland
1pm

USA (NY)
7am

USA (LA)
4am

Germany
1pm

Australia
10pm

Practicalities 177

PERSONAL SAFETY

Violent attacks on foreign tourists are very rare. Theft and pickpocketing are the most common crimes. To stay safe:

- Never leave cameras, wallets and other valuables on café tables or in unattended vehicles.
- Always lock valuable items in hotel safes.
- Beware of pickpockets in crowded areas in big cities, on trams, buses and railway stations and in particular where large numbers of foreign tourists congregate.
- Avoid walking alone at night in deserted bus stations, empty backstreets and parks.
- Avoid groups of drunks and homeless men who gather around railway stations at night.

Police assistance:
☎ **997 or 112** from mobile telephones

ELECTRICITY

 The power supply is 220 volts AC. Sockets take two-pronged round continental plugs. Visitors from the UK will need an adaptor; visitors from the US will need a transformer for 100–120 volt devices.

TELEPHONES

 There are still many public telephone boxes operated by Telekomunikacja Polska at strategic points in every village, town and city. Telephone cards (*karta* *telefoniczna*) can be bought at post offices and news kiosks. There are no coin-operated telephones. The mobile phone signal covers almost the whole of Poland. The network operators are Era, Orange, Play and Plus. Since 2007, all calls made from EU mobiles to any number within the EU are charged at a fixed standard rate. The international dialling code for Poland is 48.

Dial 00 followed by

UK:	**44**
USA/Canada	**1**
Ireland:	**353**
Australia:	**61**
Germany:	**49**

POST OFFICES

 Poland has a reliable postal system operated by Poczta Polska. Stamps are bought at post offices and at some news kiosks. Postboxes are red and marked with the word "Poczta". Letters and postcards to other EU counties usually arrive within a week and to other continents within two weeks.

TIPS/GRATUITIES

Tipping is not expected and in restaurants a service charge is included in the bill. You may want to round the bill up to the nearest 5 or 10 złoty if you are satisfied with the service.

Restaurants	Round the bill up
Taxis	No
Tour guides	5–10PLN
Porters	5PLN
Chambermaids	No
Lavatory attendants	No

	Police 997
	Fire 998
	Ambulance 999

HEALTH

 Insurance EU citizens receive free emergency medical care on production of a European Health Insurance Card (EHIC). Other nationalities should take out health insurance cover, and anyone planning to take part in sports activities, especially mountaineering, canoeing, skiing and horse riding, should take out an appropriate policy.

 Dental services Emergency dental work must be paid for and isn't always covered by private medical insurance.

 Bites Tick-borne encephalitis is spread by infected tick bites. Consider vaccination if spending long periods in woodland or camping. Mosquito bites are not dangerous but can irritate the skin. Use a DEET-based insect repellent.

 Drugs Major cities and most towns have several pharmacies (*apteka*), at least one of which will be open 24 hours. Addresses are printed in local newspapers or posted on pharmacy doors. Take adequate supplies of drugs you need on a regular basis as they may not be readily available. Other items to consider are insect repellent and anti-diarrhoea pills.

Water Tap water is safe to drink though the taste may be unpleasant. Bottled water is widely available.

CONCESSIONS

Young people Under-fours travel free on public transport, and under-12s get a 50 per cent concession. An International Student Identity Card (ISIC) entitles the holder to a discount at some tourist sights and on Warsaw's public transport system.
Senior citizens There are normally no discounts available for seniors from overseas.

TRAVELLING WITH A DISABILITY

Public transport can be a challenge for travellers with disabilities. The situation with disabled access is improving slowly, but most restaurants and hotels and many places of interest remain off limits to those with mobility problems. A handful of disabled toilets have appeared and upmarket hotels now possess good disabled facilities.

CHILDREN

Many upmarket hotels and restaurants are child-friendly with some hotels offering a babysitting service and some restaurants special child portions and highchairs. Children should be supervised at all times around Poland's dangerous roads.

TOILETS

Public toilets can be found at bus and train stations. A small charge is made to use them. Marked with a circle for women and a triangle for men.

CUSTOMS

A permit is required to export anything made before May 1945. Ask expert staff at Desa antique shops for more information.

CONSULATES

UK
282 490750

Ireland
213 929440

Canada
213 164651

Australia
213 101500

USA
217 273300

LANGUAGE

The official language in Poland is Polish, a western Slavic language which uses the Latin alphabet as opposed to the country's eastern neighbours Russia, Belarus and Ukraine, who write in Cyrillic. Polish is a phonetic language, meaning it is more or less pronounced the way it is written. Letters you won't find in English are ń (pronounced as the "ni" in "onion"), ż (pronounced as the "s" in "leisure"), ę (as in the "eng" in "engaged"), ą (as in the "ong" in "song"), ó (pronounced "u"), ł (pronounced "w" as in "water"), ś (pronounced "sh"), ć (pronounced "ch") and ź (same as ż). There are also difficult-looking combinations of letters such as sz (pronounced "sh"), cz (pronounced "ch") and rz (same as ż). Also the letter "c" is pronounced as "ts" and "ch" as in the Scottish word "loch".

GENERAL

hi/bye **zobaczenia**
hello **witam/cześć**
good morning/
 good afternoon **dzień dobry**
good evening **dobry wieczór**
good night **dobranoc**
goodbye **do widzenia**
please **proszę**
thank you **dziękuję**
you're welcome **proszę bardzo**
excuse me **przepraszam**
I'm sorry **przepraszam**
yes **tak**
no **nie**
how are you? (formal) **Jak się masz?/
 Co stychać (coll.)**
Very well, thanks **dobrze dziękuję**
I'm fine (informal) **fajno dzękuję**
cheers! **na zdrowie!**
large **wielki**
small **mały**
cheap **tani**
expensive **drogi**
Poland **Polska**
England **Anglia**
America **Ameryka**
I don't understand **Nie rozumiem**
do you speak English? **Czy pan/pani
 (m/f) mówi po angielsku?**
open **otwarte/czynne**
closed **zamknięte/nieczynne**
very **bardzo**
where? **gdzie?**
here **tu/tutaj**
there **tam**
when **kiedy**
now **teraz**
later **później**
why? **dlaczego?**
May I? Can I? **czy mogę?**
left/on the left **po lewaj/na lewo**
right/on the right **po prawej/na prawo**
today **dzisaj**
tomorrow **jutro**
Where are the toilets? **Gdzie są
 toalety?**

TRANSPORT

bus **autobus**
tram **tramwaj**
train **pociąg**
bus station **dworzec autobusowy/
 dworzec PKS**
railway station **dworzec kolejowy/
 dworzec PKP**
airport **lotnisko**
port **port**
ferry **prom**
ticket **bilet**
timetable **rozkład jazdy**
arrivals **przyjazdy**
departures **odjazdy**
taxi **taksówka**
petrol **benzyna**
Where are we? **gzie jeteśmy?**
Do I have to get off here? **Czy to mój
 przystanek?**
Where is the train/bus station? **Gdzie
 jest dworzec/dworzec autobusowy?**

SHOPPING

bakery **piekarnia**
bookshop **księgarnia**
butchers **sklep mięsny**
cake shop **cukiernia**
pharmacy **apteka**
market **targ**
How much is this? **ile ksztuje?**
Where can I buy...? **gdzie można
 kupić...**
I'm looking for... **szukam...**

MONEY

bank **bank**
exchange booth **kantor**
exchange rate **kurs**
money **pieniądze**
cash **gotówka**
banknote **banknot**
coin **moneta**
credit card **karta kredytowa**
post office **poczta**
stamp **znaczek**
postcard **kartka pocztowa**
telephone card **karta telefoniczna**
mobile phone **komórka**

ACCOMMODATION

Do you have a room? **Czy pan/pani ma pokój?**
How much per night? **Ile kosztuje za dobę?** (doba means a night and a day)
with bath/shower **z łazienką/z przysznicem**
When is breakfast served? **Która godzina jest śniadania?**

EATING OUT

A table for... please **Proszę stolik dla...**
The bill, please? **Rachunek, proszę?**
We didn't have this **Nie jedliśmy to**

CALENDAR

Monday **poniedzialek**
Tuesday **wtorek**
Wednesday **środa**
Thursday **czwartek**
Friday **piątek**
Saturday **sobota**
Sunday **niedziela**
January **styzen**
February **luty**
March **marzec**
Apri **kwiećień**
May **maj**
June **czerwiec**
July **lipiec**
August **sierpień**
September **wrzesień**
October **październik**
November **listopad**
December **grudzień**

EMERGENCIES

Help! **Pomocy!**
Stop, thief! **Łapać złodzieja**
Can you help me, please? **Proszę o pomoc?**
Call the police **Proszę zawołać policję**
Call an ambulance **Proszę zadzwonić po pogotowie**
I have lost my wallet **Zgubiłem portmonetką**
I have lost my passport **Zgubiłem paszporta**
Where is the police station? **Gdzie jest komisariat policji?**
Where is the hospital? **Gdzie jest szpital?**
I don't feel well **Źle się czuję**
first aid **pierwsza pomoc**

COLOURS

black **czarny**
brown **brązowy**
pink **różowy**
red **czerwony**
orange **pomarańczowy**
yellow **żółty**
green **zielony**
blue **niebieski**
purple **filoletowy**
white **biały**
grey **szary**

NUMBERS

0 **zero**	19 **dziewiętnaście**
1 **jeden**	20 **dwadzieścia**
2 **dwa**	21 **dwadzieścia jeden**
3 **trzy**	30 **trzydzieści**
4 **cztery**	40 **czterdzieści**
5 **pięć**	50 **pięćdziesiąt**
6 **sześć**	60 **sześćdziesiąt**
7 **siedem**	70 **siedemdziesiąt**
8 **osiem**	80 **osiemdziesiąt**
9 **dziewięć**	90 **dziewięćdziesiąt**
10 **dziesięć**	100 **sto**
11 **jedenaście**	1000 **tysiąc**
12 **dwanaście**	
13 **trzynaście**	
14 **czternaście**	
15 **piętnaście**	
16 **szesnaście**	
17 **siedemnaście**	
18 **osiemnaście**	

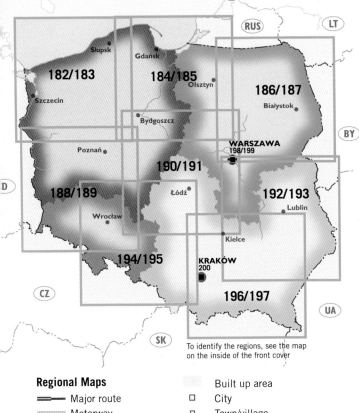

To identify the regions, see the map on the inside of the front cover

Regional Maps

===== Major route

===== Motorway

===== Dual carriageway

───── Main road

───── Secondary road

▨ Park/forest

▨ Built up area

□ City

□ Town/village

✈ Airport

▨ Featured place of interest

Streetplans

───── Main road/minor road

───── Other road

───── Railway

─●─ Tramline & stop

▨ Important building

▨ Park/garden/cemetery

▨ Featured place of interest

✝ Church

✡ Synagogue

● Metro station

ℹ Tourist information

● Monument/statue

☀ Viewpoint

182–197

| 0 | 20 km |
| 0 | 10 miles |

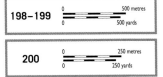

198–199

| 0 | 500 metres |
| 0 | 500 yards |

200

| 0 | 250 metres |
| 0 | 250 yards |

Atlas

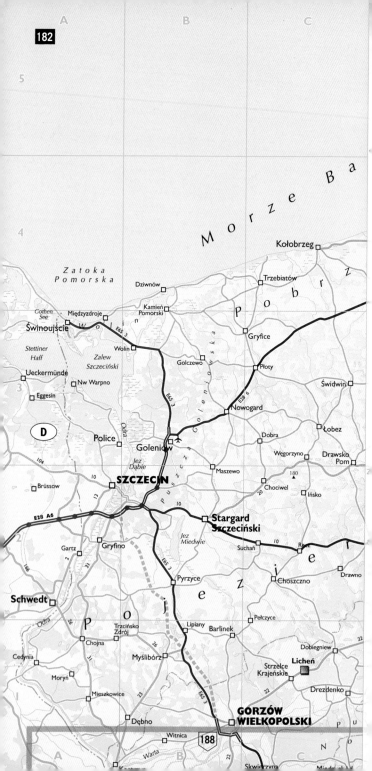

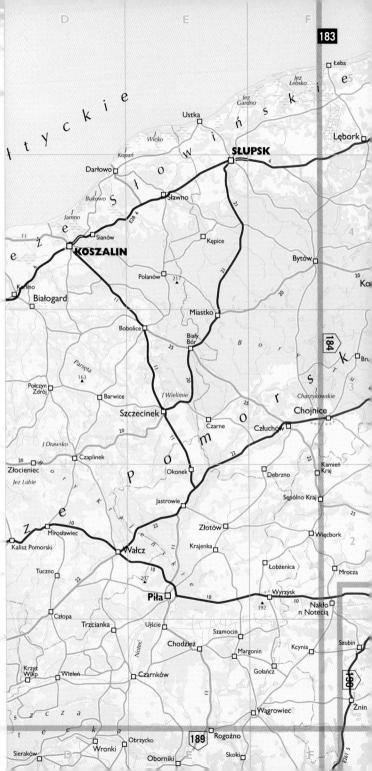

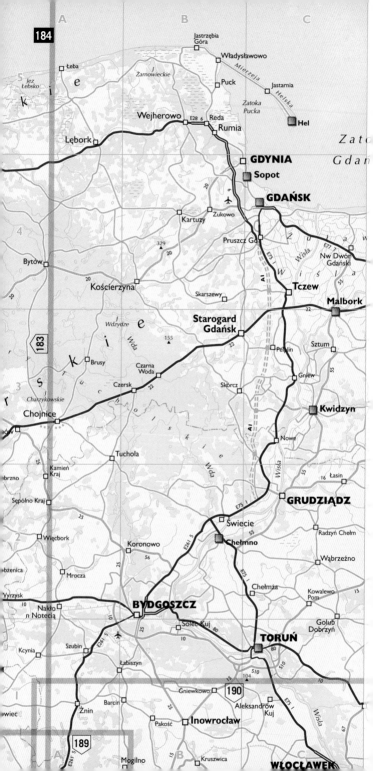

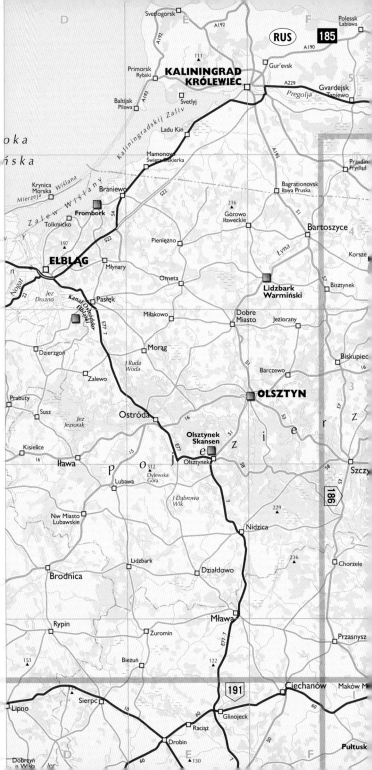

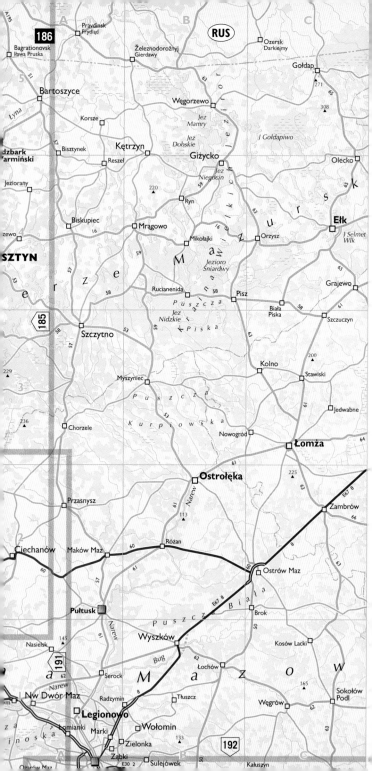

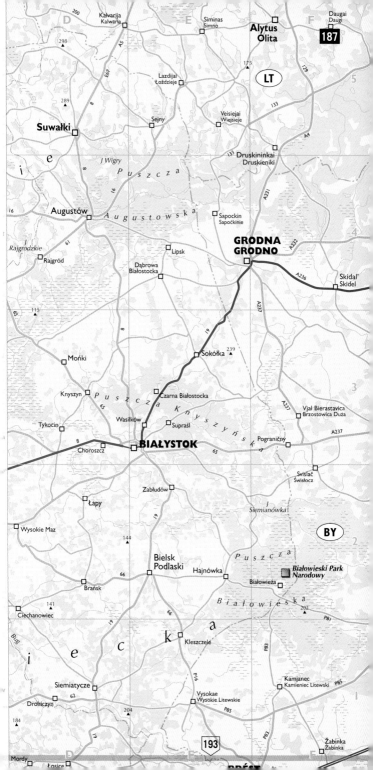

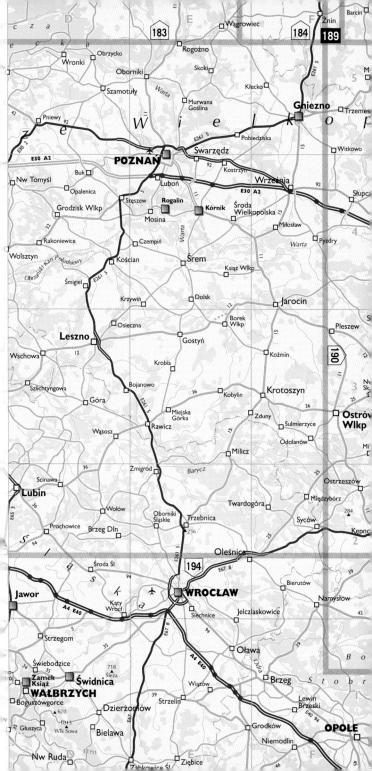

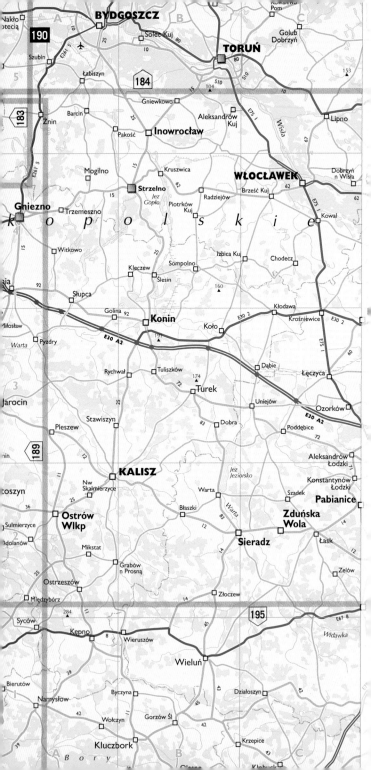

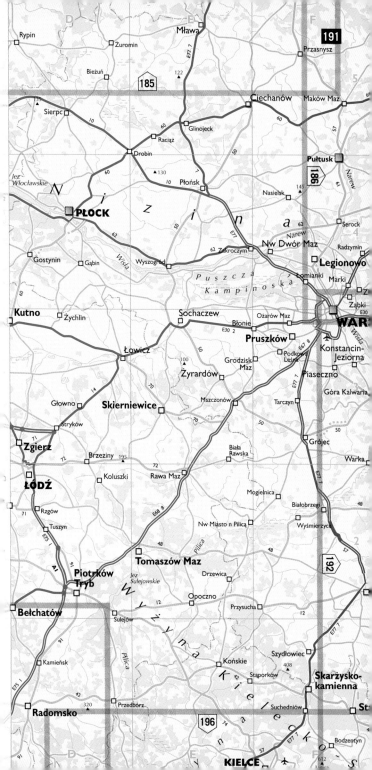

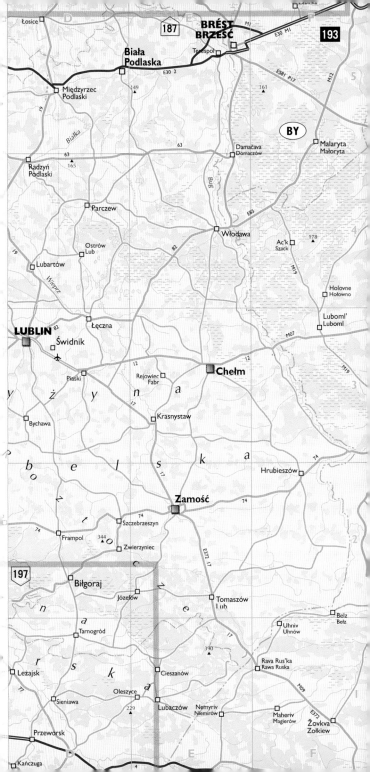

Łosice

D

187

BRÉST
BRZEŚĆ

Terespol

E30 M1

193

Biała
Podlaska

E30 2

M1

Międzyrzec
Podlaski

149

161

E581 P17

M12

5

Białka

BY

63

63

Damačava
Domaczów

Malaryta
Małoryta

Radzyń
Podlaski

165

Bug

E85

Parczew

Włodawa

Ac'k
Szack

178

4

Ostrów
Lub

82

19

Lubartów

M19

Wieprz

Holovne
Hołowno

Luboml'
Luboml

Łęczna

LUBLIN

82

M07

Świdnik

M19

12

12

Piaski

Rejowiec
Fabr

Chełm

3

n

a

Bychawa

y

ż

y

17

Krasnystaw

b

o

z

e

l

s

k

a

Hrubieszów

74

17

Zamość

74

74

Szczebrzeszyn

Frampol

344

O

z

Zwierzyniec

E372 17

197

Biłgoraj

c

Józefów

Tomaszów
Lub

e

Belz
Bełz

n

a

Tarnogród

17

Uhniv
Uhnów

390

r

s

k

Cieszanów

a

Rava Rus'ka
Rawa Ruska

Leżajsk

M09

Sieniawa

229

Oleszyce

Lubaczów

Nemyriv
Niemirów

E372

Maheriv
Magierów

Žovkva
Żołkiew

Przeworsk

D

4

E

F

1

Kańczuga

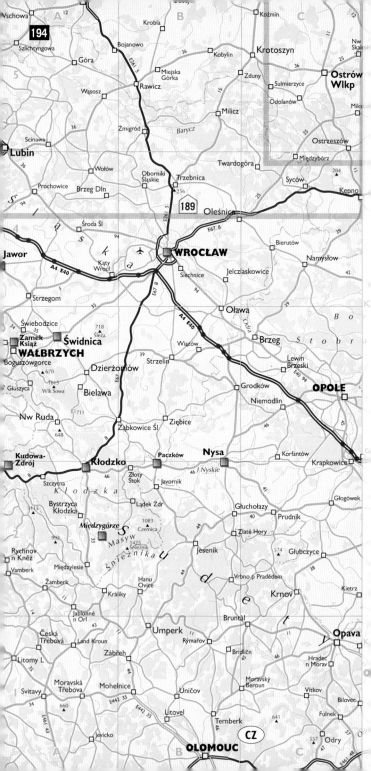